SHAPING U.S. FOREIGN POLICY

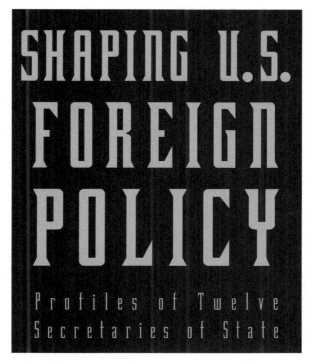

SHAPING U.S. FOREIGN POLICY

Profiles of Twelve Secretaries of State

Edward F. Dolan
Margaret M. Scariano

Democracy in Action

FRANKLIN WATTS

A Division of Grolier Publishing

New York London Hong Kong Sydney
Danbury, Connecticut

frontispiece The Great Seal of the United States in the keeping of the Secretary of State

Photographs copyright ©: United States Department of State: p. 2; Independence National Historical Park Collection: p. 12; Library of Congress: pp. 15, 22; New York Public Library Picture Collection: pp. 28, 37, 47, 69, 84, 89; Jay Mallin: pp. 55, 63; United Nations: p. 65; UPI/Bettmann: pp. 76, 81.

Library of Congress Cataloging-in-Publication Data

Dolan, Edward F., 1924–
    Shaping U.S. foreign policy: profiles of twelve secretaries of state / Edward F. Dolan, Margaret M. Scariano.
        p.   cm. — (Democracy in action (Franklin Watts, inc.))
    Includes bibliographical references and index.
    Summary: Profiles five secretaries of state who made major acquisitions of land and seven secretaries who dealt with the search for peace or with the Cold War.
    ISBN 0-531-11264-0
    1. United States — Foreign relations — Juvenile literature. 2. Cabinet officers — United States — Biography — Juvenile literature. 3. Statesman — United States — Biography — Juvenile literature. [1. United States — Foreign relations. 2. Cabinet officers. 3. Statesman.] I. Scariano, Margaret. II. Title. III. Series.
    E183.7.D65   1996
    327.73 — dc20   95-49390 CIP AC

··· CONTENTS ···

one

MEET THE SECRETARY OF STATE
•••

On April 30, 1789, when George Washington took office as the first president of the United States, he shouldered a variety of tasks as the infant nation's chief executive: he had to keep track of its finances; as commander in chief of the armed services, he bore the responsibility for the country's defense; and he had to manage the government's relations with foreign nations.

Though the United States was but a fraction of the size it is today, Washington recognized a hard fact. In his words, the number of tasks pointed up "the impossibility that one man should be able to perform all the great business of the state."[1]

As a result, he immediately established three departments to assist him and named the men who would head them. He was empowered to do so by Article 1 in Section II of the Constitution. The article did not name the departments but left it to the president to decide exactly which offices and men were needed.

The three departments that took shape were the Departments of Treasury, War, and the subject of this book, State.

Named respectively to head them were the shrewd financial expert Alexander Hamilton; the trusted and hardworking artilleryman of the Revolutionary War, Henry Knox; and the brilliant redheaded statesman who had penned much of the Declaration of Independence, Thomas Jefferson.[2]

These three men became the first appointees to what is today known as the president's cabinet. Washington did not christen the group with that name then, however. It was not used until 1793, when it was coined by the Virginian who would become the nation's fourth president, James Madison.[3]

Over the past two centuries, the cabinet has grown to a membership of thirteen. Today, it is manned by the secretaries of state, treasury, defense, interior, agriculture, commerce and labor, housing and human development, transportation, energy, health and human services, education, veterans affairs, and the attorney general.

It has always been traditional for a president to select his cabinet members, who are then routinely approved by Congress. Cabinet members work at the sole discretion of the president. He is free not only to hire but also to discharge any of their number.[4]

Ever since the position was established, the secretary of state has served as the cabinet's ranking officer because, since he deals with nations throughout the world, his duties are especially wide-ranging. As the cabinet's ranking member, he stands fourth in the line of presidential succession. Should the president ever be unable to serve, his post passes to the vice president. If there is further difficulty, the presidency falls, in turn, to the speaker of the House of Representatives, the president pro tempore of the Senate, and then the secretary of state.

The Secretary of State

The secretary of state heads the U.S. Department of State and is charged with assisting the president in five ways. Working with the chief executive,

1. the secretary develops and implements foreign policy, which consists of the nation's aims and decisions in its dealings with other countries;
2. the secretary communicates with other countries on behalf of the United States;
3. the secretary maintains United States representatives in nations across the world;
4. the secretary negotiates foreign treaties and agreements; and
5. the secretary supervises and coordinates the work of the United States with international bodies, such as the United Nations.[5]

As head of today's Department of State, the secretary is responsible for the work of 24,000 employees—a number that would surely surprise Thomas Jefferson. When he got down to work in 1789, he was given a staff of five clerks, two messengers, and a part-time translator of French (which was used by diplomats to avoid the problems posed by the world's various languages). He founded several diplomatic offices in cities overseas—including London and Paris—and stood ready to negotiate his country's business and treaties with all nations.

Jefferson was also charged with a variety of domestic duties. His staff took the census, granted patents, and issued passports. Being the first to serve in the office, he had to organize his department and put it to work with an annual budget of less than 10,000 dollars.

How things have changed since Jefferson's time! Today, in countries both large and small, the State Department maintains some 115 embassies and 120 consular offices. The work of the consular and diplomatic services puzzles many people. The two are often thought to be the same thing. Consular offices are established abroad to promote trade with the United States, protect the rights of visiting and resident American citizens, and provide visas that enable foreign nationals to enter the United States. Diplomatic services include handling official negotiations with governments abroad and the maintaining of political, economic, and social ties with foreign countries.

In addition, the department also supervises special units that work with such bodies as the United Nations and the North Atlantic Treaty Organization (NATO). NATO was established in 1949 and is an association of nations that are pledged to defend Europe against any enemy (principally at that time, the Soviet bloc).

Further, the department maintains offices for handling specific tasks. Some deal with economic, educational, cultural, and scientific matters of international import while others supervise the security of diplomatic and consular posts. Still others attend to congressional relations, and some handle public and press information.

Finally, a number of individual agencies are either a part of the State Department or function in cooperation with it. One is the United States Information Agency, which was established in 1953 to beam radio programs overseas for the purpose of informing and influencing public opinion there; though it is an independent office, its director coordinates its policies and plans with the secretary of state. Another is the much admired Peace Corps. Formed in 1961 during president John F. Kennedy's administration, it provides skilled volunteers to help in the economic, educational, and cultural development of interested foreign countries. It is a separate agency that is located within and under the supervision of the State Department.

In all, the department deals on a twenty-four-hour-a-day basis with foreign governments everywhere, international organizations, and the American people.

The Secretaries of State: A Varied History

To date, sixty-one men have served as secretary of state.[6] Their histories in office have varied greatly. The work of some has contributed mightily to the territorial growth of the United States.

For example, the energetic William H. Seward, who served under Presidents Abraham Lincoln and Andrew Johnson, promoted and then negotiated the purchase of Alaska from Russia in 1867. The purchase was widely opposed by the public. Nationwide, the acquisition was dubbed "Seward's folly."

Other secretaries won their places in history for the significant treaties they arranged. High on the list of their number is John M. Hay. As secretary under president Theodore Roosevelt at the dawn of the twentieth century, he negotiated the treaties with Great Britain and Panama that led to the construction of the Panama Canal, an engineering feat that enhanced global trade as never before by carving a fifty-one-mile path between the Atlantic and Pacific oceans.

Many, as did Secretary George C. Marshall, increased the prestige of the United States worldwide. While serving for President Harry S. Truman in the late 1940s, he devised the European Recovery Program. Under the program, the United States contributed its mighty resources to the rebuilding of a Europe left in ruins by World War Two. The program is remembered worldwide as the Marshall Plan.

And still others played major roles in the Cold War, which erupted in the wake of World War Two and lasted until the dawn of the 1990s. It was an intense political and ideological struggle that, short of open war, pitted the Soviet Union and the world's Communist countries against the United States and its fellow democracies. A dozen secretaries served during that four-decade period of global upheaval. Among them was John Foster Dulles, who joined President Dwight D. Eisenhower in bringing an end to a conflict that turned the Cold War hot for three years in the 1950s—the Korean War.

In this book we will look at the history of the secretary of state by telling the stories of twelve secretaries. They are considered to be among the most illustrious of all who have served in the post. To read their stories is to follow the course of American history.

We begin in the early 1800s with a man who weighed little more than 100 pounds but stands as a giant in our history. His name was James Madison.

··· Thomas Jefferson, the first secretary of state and the third
president of the United States ···

JAMES MADISON AND NAPOLEON'S BARGAIN

• • •

In little more than two centuries, the United States has changed from a collection of thirteen former British colonies along the Atlantic seaboard to a nation that stretches not only from "sea to shining sea" but also beyond. Its growth has involved the addition of many land holdings. Some were purchased; some were gained by annexation; some were brought about by treaty.

One of the greatest of those acquisitions—for one of the best prices in the history of the country—was made soon after Thomas Jefferson entered the White House in 1801 to serve as the nation's third president. At the time, the United States stretched down the Atlantic coast from Maine to the northern border of Florida, westward to the Mississippi River, and south along the river to a point north of the Gulf of Mexico. The rest of the continent—easily two-thirds of its land mass—was held by France, Spain, Russia, and Britain.

Though the United States occupied but a small portion of the continent, the new president, in his inaugural address, declared that the young nation had all the land it would need for a thousand generations.[1] He was soon to change his mind.

Events led him to the nation's first land acquisition—the purchase of the vast Louisiana Territory from France. It was a purchase that ranked high on the list of accomplishments of the man who served as Jefferson's secretary of state and then went on to become the country's fourth president—James Madison.

James Madison

Born March 16, 1751, on a Virginia plantation that grew tobacco and grains, James Madison was the oldest of twelve children.[2] A sickly and weak child, he grew into a shy and reserved man who stood only five feet four inches tall and weighed barely more than 100 pounds.

But despite his shyness and delicate health, Madison was an energetic and ambitious man who was to carve for himself a distinguished career in public service. That career began in 1774 when, after studying law at the College of New Jersey (now Princeton University), he entered the Virginia political scene to serve on the Orange County Committee of Safety and then win election as a delegate to the Virginia Convention of 1776. The convention voted in favor of independence from Britain and drafted a new Virginia constitution.

Three years later, in the midst of the Revolutionary War, he was elected to the Continental Congress. During his first stay there, which lasted until 1783, Madison vigorously supported the idea of a strong national government for the newborn United States. His finest early work, however, began to take shape in 1787 when he served as a delegate to the Constitutional Convention at Philadelphia. He argued eloquently in favor of the governmental structure that remains to this day: the division of the federal government into three branches—a strong executive branch, an independent federal court system, and a bicameral (two houses) legislature—that provide a system of checks and balances that keeps any one of the three from gaining too much power.

Madison went on to help draft the nation's constitution and worked tirelessly—speaking and writing and drawing on all

··· James Madison ···

his reserves of energy—to gain its ratification by the states. For these efforts he earned the title "The Father of the Constitution."

He then returned to Congress in 1789 and took a leading role in drafting the legislation necessary for organizing the government under the new Constitution. Of even greater importance, he proposed the nine amendments to the Constitution that served as the basis for the Bill of Rights.

Thomas Jefferson, on assuming the presidency, immediately named Madison as his secretary of state. From the beginning, the two men worked well together because Madison was not only the president's trusted and influential adviser but his close and respected friend as well. Jefferson consulted with him on all important decisions, and many of the administration's new ideas and policies came from Madison.

Madison's duties as secretary proved vastly different from those he had shouldered as a congressman. Instead of speeches, debates, and votes on various measures, he was now responsible for an enormous amount of official correspondence with foreign leaders and America's representatives abroad. There was also a great change in his social life.

Jefferson made Madison and his wife, Dolley, an integral part of the Washington social scene. Because the president was a widower, he had Dolley serve as hostess at White House gatherings. For Dolley, this was no task. Seventeen years younger than Madison, she was a lively, spirited beauty who greatly enjoyed parties. Not only did she assist Jefferson socially but also did much to alter her husband's shy manner. Her vivacity brought Madison out of his "shell" and he learned to revel in the White House festivities. He acquired a reputation for being a warm and intelligent man who sparked his conversation with amusing anecdotes.

Madison and the Louisiana Purchase

During his first term as secretary, Madison was deeply concerned about the city of New Orleans.[3] It lay near the southern end of the Mississippi River. The river formed the eastern border of the vast Louisiana Territory and was vital to American trade. It served as the main highway for boats and barges carrying merchandise to the Gulf of Mexico for shipment to the markets of the world.

The Louisiana Territory, which spread west to the Rocky Mountains, was held by Spain at the close of the 1700s. For years Spain had allowed Americans to sail their goods down the Mississippi to New Orleans. There a shipper could store them temporarily in warehouses without paying special taxes as long as they were not to be sent on to Spanish holdings. But everything abruptly changed about a year and half before Jefferson won the presidency. In 1799 Napoleon Bonaparte installed himself as the ruler of France. He immediately exacted from a weak Spain a treaty that handed him the Louisiana Territory. In doing so, he took back an old French holding that had been ceded to Spain in the 1760s.

Napoleon's Plan for a New World Empire

Napoleon wanted the vast expanse of the Louisana Territory for a specific reason. He intended to take control of the Caribbean island of Hispaniola. Today the home of the Dominican Republic and Haiti, the island was to serve as the base of operations for an offensive that would establish a French empire in the New World. One of the major targets in that conquest lay within the Louisiana Territory—the sprawling Mississippi Valley. Napoleon planned to use it as a food and trade center for his New World empire.

The western end of Hispaniola, which had been a French possession since the 1600s, still belonged to France—but in name only. In 1793 a native soldier-statesman, Francois Toussaint L'Ouverture, had led a successful slave revolt that toppled the local French colonial government. Then, though Toussaint did not declare Hispaniola an independent nation, he ruled the island with hardly a nod toward France. So Napoleon, as the first step along the road to his New World empire, set about overthrowing L'Ouverture and recapturing Hispaniola. To accomplish this task, he sent 20,000 troops into the Caribbean.

The Campaign to Buy New Orleans

The situation alarmed both Jefferson and Madison. With the French controlling the Louisiana Territory, the United States would lose the Mississippi River as a trade route and New Orleans as a depository for goods under shipment. The young and militarily weak United States would have to go to war to oust the French and regain access to the Mississippi.

A war with a mighty power promised disaster for the country. Jefferson and Madison could think of only one way to avoid such a fate and at the same time strengthen America's position on the Mississippi: buy New Orleans and a surrounding tract of land from Napoleon. With New Orleans in U.S. hands, the nation would still have a southern port to which goods could be shipped overland.

Madison instructed Robert Livingston, the United States minister to France, to offer Napoleon ten million dollars for the purchase. If Napoleon turned down the offer, Livingston was to attempt to win free navigation of the Mississippi for American shippers.

While Livingston talked in Paris, Madison wrote lengthy legal arguments to help the American convince Napoleon to approve the sale. The president felt certain that the Frenchman would be reluctant to sell because of his plans for the part it would play in his New World empire. Jefferson sent James Monroe, his close friend who would become the nation's fifth president, to France to join in the negotiations.

An Odd Turn of Events

Suddenly, in the midst of the negotiations, American history took one of its oddest turns. While Monroe was crossing the Atlantic, Napoleon told Livingston that he was willing to sell not only New Orleans but the entire expanse of the Louisiana Territory. Two reasons were behind his surprise offer. First, his invasion of Hispaniola had gone badly. His troops had overthrown L'Ouverture after long fighting, only to fall prey to an insidious enemy, yellow fever. Thousands of their number had died of the disease and had ended the French leader's hopes for a New World empire.

Second, in his attempts to conquer all of Europe, he was about to renew his war with Britain, which had been stalled for twenty months. But he knew that British sea power far exceeded his, and he feared that, should he be defeated, the English would likely demand that he turn the Louisiana Territory over to them. Consequently, he elected to sell the vast expanse to the United States and use the money for his European military activities, hoping that America, with the Louisiana Territory in its hands, would become a major power that could thwart British colonial ambitions in the New World.

The French leader's sudden offer stunned and delighted Jefferson and Madison. Napoleon was willing to take fifteen million dollars for the entire Louisiana Territory—just five million dollars more than the Americans had said they would pay for the New Orleans tract, which was the size of a tiny farm in comparison. It was the bargain of all bargains!

Jefferson wasted no time in accepting the offer, and the treaties for the Louisiana Purchase were signed on April 30, 1803, and were ratified by Congress on the following October 20. Into American hands came an expanse of fertile and mineral-rich land that doubled the size of the nation and would one day embrace all or part of thirteen new states: all of Arkansas, Missouri, Iowa, South Dakota, and Nebraska; virtually all of Louisiana; and parts of Minnesota, North Dakota, Montana, Wyoming, Kansas, Oklahoma, and Colorado.

At the time of the purchase, the exact size of the territory was unknown. The future years showed it to cover some 828,000 square miles. At a price of fifteen million dollars, its cost broke down to a mere three cents per acre.

The Louisiana Purchase was the first of America's major land acquisitions. More were to come in the following years.

three

JOHN QUINCY ADAMS AND THE MONROE DOCTRINE

•••

The term *foreign policy* refers to a nation's philosophies, aims, and decisions in its dealings with foreign countries. Ever since 1823, a cornerstone of U.S. foreign policy has been the Monroe Doctrine, which was named for America's fifth president, James Monroe. Though Monroe announced the doctrine, it was very much the result of behind-the-scenes work by one of the most brilliant secretaries of state, John Quincy Adams.

John Quincy Adams

The son of John Adams, the nation's second president, John Quincy Adams was born in Braintree (now Quincy), Massachusetts, on July 11, 1767. As an adult, he weighed around 175 pounds and stood five feet seven inches tall. With his piercing black eyes and heavy eyebrows, he was considered a handsome man.[1]

His looks, however, belied an aloof and austere manner. His political opponents accused him of having a gloomy dislike of mankind, and his political enemies compared him to an "unsocial savage." Nevertheless, he proved to be a master of the art of negotiations and was considered one of the finest diplomats of his time. He also recorded one of the longest marriages of any secretary. At age thirty, he married twenty-two-year-old Louisa Catherine Johnson, a sickly woman who was famous for ailments ranging from migraine headaches to fainting spells. Regardless of his gloomy ways and her complaints of delicate health, their union lasted for fifty-one years and produced four children.

Adams's diplomatic career began while he was still a child. He was just eleven when he accompanied his father on a diplomatic mission to France and served as the elder Adams's secretary. While there, he gave English lessons to the French minister and his secretary. The next year saw him acting as secretary and interpreter to diplomat Francis Dana on America's first mission to the Russian court at St. Petersburg. Adams had an exceptional talent for languages and was known to have spoken five or six modern tongues as well as Latin and Greek.

On returning from Europe in 1785, he entered Harvard College, graduated in 1787, and went on to study law for two years before going into practice in Boston. Within a few years, though, he was recalled to government service. Three of America's first four presidents took advantage of his diplomatic and linguistic skills.

George Washington sent him as American minister to the Netherlands in 1794 because he was one of the few Americans fluent in Dutch. Then, beginning in 1797, he served as a diplomat in Russia for four years while his father was in the White House. On returning home, he won election as a U.S. senator from Massachusetts and strongly supported the Louisiana Purchase. But he was back overseas in 1809—sent this time by James Madison to serve as America's minister to Russia.

In 1814 Madison named him to head the U.S. delegation that traveled to Belgium to negotiate the Treaty of Ghent with the British. The pact ended the War of 1812. The next year, Adams settled in London for a two-year stint as the American minister to Britain.

··· John Quincy Adams ···

When James Monroe entered the White House in 1817, he summoned Adams home and named him secretary of state. It was a post for which Adams, with his background in diplomacy, proved to be well suited.

In 1818 Adams negotiated a treaty with Britain that set the American-Canadian border along a line at 49° north latitude between the Great Lakes and the Rocky Mountains. The treaty also called for the border to be demilitarized by both the United States and Britain (an arrangement that remains to this day) and secured U.S. fishing rights off certain Canadian coasts. Then, the next year, he played a major role in America's acquisition of the Spanish holding that, shaped like an inverted L, eventually became the state of Florida.

Florida Joins the United States

The story of that acquisition involved violence by Seminole Indians, runaway slaves, and cattle rustlers who charged over the Florida border into America's Louisiana Territory to attack and rob the people there and then escape back to the safety of Florida.

Soon after becoming secretary of state, Adams approached Don Luis de Onis, the Spanish minister to Washington, and asked about the possibility of purchasing Florida. De Onis was interested, but the negotiations came to a halt when President Monroe, outraged at the latest attacks on the people of Louisiana, instructed General Andrew Jackson, the commander of the American troops on the Louisiana-Florida border, to wipe out the invaders and, *if necessary,* to enter Florida itself. The general, whose toughness was reflected in his nickname, "Old Hickory," interpreted these instructions as an order to invade. He crashed into the Spanish territory, captured two forts, and hanged two Englishmen who had been furnishing the Seminoles with arms and inciting them to violence.

Jackson's raid created a furor in Monroe's cabinet. Secretary of War John C. Calhoun charged that the general had exceeded his White House orders and had illegally invaded a foreign nation's holding. Further, Jackson had infuriated the British government by hanging the two Englishmen. He needed to be severely disciplined. With one exception, the cabinet supported Calhoun. That exception was Adams. Rigorously defending Jackson's raid, he argued that the United States had been justified in taking drastic measures to protect its people in Louisiana. He won the cabinet over and saved Old Hickory a humiliating censure. Then, blunt and flinty as ever, he told Spain that it had violated American rights by not stopping the outlaw raids into the Louisiana Territory.

Jackson's capture of the two Florida forts proved to Spain that America had the strength to take the region by force. Consequently, the Spanish agreed to Adams's proposal that the territory be ceded to the United States. Facing Spain at that time were claims by Americans for damages suffered in the forays into Louisiana. They amounted to five million dollars. The United States agreed to pay the claims, sending the payments directly to the Americans and not passing them through Spain. The agreement brought more than 54,000 square miles of territory into the American fold and rounded out the nation's southeastern border.

Adams and the Monroe Doctrine

By 1820, U.S. foreign policy had two main goals: first, to remove potential foreign enemies from the North American continent by buying their holdings and, second, in keeping with the advice in Washington's farewell address, to avoid entanglements in European affairs.[2]

But now an event occurred in Europe that was to add a new viewpoint to the nation's foreign policy and become its cornerstone—the Monroe Doctrine. That event was the formation of the Holy Alliance. The Alliance came into being when Austria, Prussia, and Russia—later to be joined by France—agreed that the great powers in Europe had the right to suppress revolutionary actions that sought to overthrow any government. As a result, Austrian troops quelled a revolution in Italy and French forces stamped out an uprising in Spain. Then, when Spain lamented the loss of its American holdings—not only Florida but Latin American colonies as well—the alliance countries agreed to help it regain the territory and, in the process, help themselves to some additional New World land. France coveted Mexico, while Russia hoped to push south from its Alaska holding to California.

These plans alarmed the United States. England, too, was disturbed and opposed the aggressive plans because trade with the Latin American nations was a profitable one. George Canning, the British foreign minister, proposed that the United States and Britain join in warning the Alliance to keep its hands off the Western Hemisphere. Canning also urged that Britain and the United States pledge not to seek further territories for themselves in the hemisphere.

President Monroe consulted with former presidents Jefferson and Madison on the proposal. Both recommended that it be accepted because it would strengthen the ties between America and Britain. In addition, they said, the powerful British fleet might well inhibit the ambitions of any nation with its eye on the New World.

Monroe's cabinet, with the single exception of John Quincy Adams, agreed with this approach. Adams vehemently objected, first because he had no wish to bind the United States to an agreement that would shut the door on the nation's future land acquisitions on the North American continent. Second, he believed it would be cowardly to entrust the safety of the Americas to the British navy—in his words, to follow along like "a cockboat in the wake of the British man-of-war." Adams insisted that the country should have the courage to issue its own declaration and work toward establishing democracies in the Western hemisphere.

Monroe heeded his feisty secretary's advice. With Adams leading the way, the two men hammered out a foreign policy that the president presented to Congress in 1823. The policy was a simple but consequential one. It held that the American continents were no longer subject to foreign colonization. Further, because the European and American systems of government were different and separate, the United States would consider any attempt to establish the European system in the Western Hemisphere as a hostile act. Conversely, the United States would stay out of Europe's internal affairs and would take no part in European wars.

The policy became known as the Monroe Doctrine. It was destined to serve as a basic creed for America's dealings with foreign nations. Adams was credited with leading the way to its formation and providing a major share of the thinking that went into it.

Adams went on to serve as secretary for Monroe's two terms. In 1825 he won election as the nation's sixth president and remained in the White House for one term. He died at age eighty, with his career in public service spanning an astonishing seventy years.

In the coming chapters, we'll see that the Monroe Doctrine, as a mainstay of American foreign policy, has been called into use on a number of occasions through the years. The first secretary of state to employ it was James Buchanan.

f o u r

JAMES BUCHANAN, OREGON COUNTRY, AND A WAR WITH MEXICO

• • •

Three land acquisitions in the 1840s all but rounded out the continental limits of the United States. Secured by the nation were Oregon Country, Texas, and the vast Mexican-owned tract known as New Mexico. All three acquisitions were made within a span of just three years. Playing a major role in bringing them about was the secretary of state at that time, James Buchanan, who served under President James K. Polk and then advanced to the White House a few years later.

James Buchanan

James Buchanan was one of the very few secretaries—six in all—who advanced to the presidency, the others being Thomas Jefferson, James Madison, James Monroe, John Quincy Adams, and Martin van Buren.[1] All were elected the nation's chief executive in the 1800s. No secretary has gone on to the White House in the twentieth century.

··· James Buchanan ···

Buchanan also holds the distinction of being the only bachelor ever to live in the White House. When he was twenty-eight years old, he became engaged to Anne C. Coleman, the daughter of a wealthy family. The couple quarreled and broke the engagement. Neither was willing to take the first step toward reconciliation until the separation was made permanent by Anne's death, thought to be a suicide. Grief-stricken, Buchanan wrote Anne's father asking to view her remains and accompany the family to the graveside. His letter was returned unopened. For the rest of his life, he was courteous to women but never showed a romantic interest in them.

Born in a Pennsylvania log cabin on April 23, 1791, Buchanan was the oldest of eight children. His father was a country storekeeper. His mother, a self-educated woman, encouraged and guided the education of her children. Buchanan credited her for much of his later success.

In adulthood, Buchanan stood just over six feet tall. He was a fair-skinned man with blue eyes and a high forehead. Throughout his life, he was an avid reader, despite the fact that he was a victim of "wryneck," a condition caused by one eye being nearsighted and the other farsighted. To see clearly, he had to keep his head cocked to the left at all times.

A lawyer by profession (he was admitted to the bar in 1812 after graduating from Pennsylvania's Dickinson College and studying under attorney James Hopkins), Buchanan entered politics in 1814. Ahead of him lay a career of more than forty years—a career that would take him from the Pennsylvania House of Representatives to the White House. Along the way, he won elections to the U.S. House of Representatives and the U.S. Senate and served for a time as America's minister to Russia.

When James K. Polk was elected the nation's eleventh president, he appointed Buchanan his secretary of state. It was a wise choice because of Buchanan's background in foreign affairs. Not only had he served as Minister to Russia but had also headed the Senate's Foreign Relations Committee. But he found himself unable to formulate as much foreign policy as he had hoped. Polk had other work for him to do.

The president was a strong advocate of the American view known as *Manifest Destiny.* Widely popular in the early 1800s, it held that the nation had the right and the duty to expand westward to the Pacific coast. And so he wanted his secretary to accomplish three tasks—secure the sole ownership of Oregon Country, Texas, and the New Mexico region.

Buchanan and Oregon Country

In 1818, on the basis of explorations and settlement by the United States and Britain, the two countries agreed to the joint ownership of Oregon Country. The region stretched up the Pacific coast from today's state of Oregon to Canada's British Columbia and onward to the southern edge of Alaska, which was then occupied by Russians and known as Russian America.[2]

By the time of Polk's election, the American population in Oregon Country far exceeded that of the English. Consequently, Polk and his fellow believers in Manifest Destiny felt that America had a right to claim the region. Further, the president and his secretary of state invoked the Monroe Doctrine to justify the U.S. claim. In May 1846, with the support of Congress, Polk notified Britain that the 1818 joint-ownership agreement was to be terminated. At first, the termination did not worry the British too much. They had used the region in great part for fur trapping and trading and considered it to be just about "furred out."

But then Polk announced that Oregon Country belonged to the United States up to the boundary of 54° 40' north latitude, the line that had been urged for several years by Manifest Destiny advocates. However, if set at that latitude, the American border would slice across the present-day Canadian province of British Columbia, so the proposal was sure to anger Britain.

It did. The British charged that the United States had no valid claim to land north of the Columbia River (in today's Oregon). The dispute held the threat of war and alarmed Secretary Buchanan. Though he had originally supported the American claim, he now backtracked and sought to calm everyone through compromise. As a result, he negotiated a treaty with Britain that—when signed in June 1846, and then approved by Congress—divided Oregon Country along a line at 49° north latitude, or, as the line was called, the forty-ninth parallel. The area south of the line went to the United States while the area to the north went to British Canada.

The setting of the line completed a work that was begun in 1818, when John Quincy Adams had arranged with the British to stretch the American-Canadian border along the forty-ninth parallel from a point near the Great Lakes west to the Rocky Mountains. The border now extended out to the Pacific coast.

According to the treaty, Vancouver Island, even though it extended below the forty-ninth parallel, was left to the British. Both countries still had the use of the Strait of Juan de Fuca— the passageway that ran between Vancouver Island and the present-day state of Washington—and Britain had the right to navigate the American-held Columbia River.

In addition to the region being pretty well "furred out," there were two reasons why Britain agreed to the compromise. First, there was the matter of population. More than 5,000 Americans had settled in the Willamette Valley (in today's Oregon), while only 750 Britishers had made their homes north of the Columbia River. If a dispute over the boundary led to a confrontation between the two groups, it would certainly end in disaster for the outnumbered Britishers. Second, if the dispute led to open warfare with the United States, British experts felt that Oregon Country could not be defended.

Once the treaty took effect, Oregon Country was given a new name—the Oregon Territory. Today the region, covering more than 165,000 square miles, is home to Oregon and Washington.

Buchanan, Texas, and New Mexico

It was a relieved Buchanan who saw the treaty signed and approved. His compromise had avoided a war with Britain and had rounded out the northwestern boundaries of the United States. Now President Polk turned him to his next task: the acquisition of Texas and adjacent New Mexico—the vast expanse of Mexican-owned land that spread north and west from Texas out to the rich province of California on the Pacific coast.[3]

When Polk entered the White House in early 1845, the Mexican government claimed ownership of Texas. But it was an ownership that was in question. This was because the American settlers there had successfully rebelled against Mexico in 1836 and had established a republic for themselves. Now, for close to ten years, they had conducted their own affairs with no interference from Mexico. Despite contending that it still owned Texas, the Mexican government had never made an effort to recapture the area.

Immediately after Polk's election but before he actually moved into the White House, Congress invited Texas to become a state in the Union, in great part because southern legislators wanted it to be admitted as a slave state and thus increase their power. The Texans favored joining the United States, but Mexico, though it had shown no interest in Texas for a decade, was outraged and broke off diplomatic relations with the United States in early 1846. Such breaks were usually the prelude to war.

Polk, with Buchanan at his side, had no desire for a fight with Mexico and attempted to settle the matter peaceably. He sent envoy James Slidell to Mexico City with an offer to pay five million dollars not only for Texas but also for the New Mexico region. In addition, he offered to pay all damages that the Americans in Texas claimed were due to them from Mexico as a result of the fighting that led to the founding of their republic. Mexico coldly refused the offer.

At the time, Texas held that its southern border ran along the Rio Grande River, an idea that the Mexicans found ridiculous, arguing that such a boundary was far too deep inside their own land. They sent troops to the Rio Grande to give muscle to their argument. Polk responded by dispatching an army force under General Zachary Taylor to a point near the river to protect what he said would be the western boundary of the United States if Texas joined the Union. Taylor, however, advanced beyond that point to the Rio Grande itself. A contingent of Mexican troops charged across the waterway and attacked Taylor's troops. A total of sixteen Americans were wounded or killed in the fighting.

A fight with Mexico now seemed inevitable. Secretary Buchanan drafted a speech that the president delivered on May 13, 1846, asking Congress to declare war on Mexico. Congress approved the request.

The Mexican War lasted for two years and caused a sharp division of opinion among the Americans. Among those who favored the conflict were the expansionists and the pioneers who wanted to move into Texas but were afraid to do so unless the area was under the American flag. Opponents knew Mexico to be a weak and poor nation and looked on the war as a dishonorable action—a barefaced land grab by a much stronger country.

The war was fought on three fronts. On one front, Taylor crossed the Rio Grande into northern Mexico. On another, a U.S. force commanded by General Winfield Scott struck central Mexico from the Gulf of Mexico and battled its way to Mexico City, the nation's capital. On still another, troops under the command of General Stephen Kearny advanced overland from Texas to the far western province of California.

Secretary Buchanan played a behind-the-scenes role in the move against California. He sent secret messages to Thomas Larkin, the American consul in the province, urging him to support any revolutionary movement there and to do all in his power to convince the Americans in California to break with Mexico and set up a government of their own. He also encouraged Larkin to lead the Californians into asking that the province be made part of the United States.

And, indeed, there was a revolutionary movement in California. When Kearny's army reached its destination, he found that the province had already been much subdued by a rebel group led by explorer John C. Fremont and a naval fleet commanded by Commodore John Sloat. With Sloat, Kearny a large

Mexican force in the Battle of the San Gabriel River in January 1847, and brought all of California under U.S. control.

The war ended in February 1848, with the signing of the Treaty of Guadaloupe Hidalgo, which was approved by Congress the following month. Mexico agreed to the Rio Grande as the southern boundary of Texas and ceded to the United States both Texas and the New Mexico tract, including California. In all, the United States gained some 918,000 square miles of territory—exceeding by more than 90,000 square miles the amount of land won in the Louisiana Purchase. The acquisition gave the nation all of today's California, Nevada, and Utah; most of present-day Arizona; parts of Colorado, New Mexico, and Wyoming; and additions to Texas. For this territory, the United States, although it had won it in battle, agreed to pay fifteen million dollars and to assume payment for the damages said to be owed to them by the Texans. In great part, this gesture was made to ease the public condemnation that the government had suffered in waging the war. The payment of the damages came to over three million dollars.

Texas was formally annexed into the United States and became a state in December 1845, just before the outbreak of the Mexican War. California joined the Union in 1853.

Secretary Buchanan did not arrange the Treaty of Guadaloupe Hidalgo. That task fell to Nicholas Trist, President Polk's envoy to Mexico. But Buchanan, because of his role as an influential advisor to the president, is given much credit for the acquisitions of Texas and New Mexico, and, in particular, for the winning of Oregon Country. While he was in office, the nation all but rounded out the land that would become the contiguous forty-eight states.

The Gadsden Purchase

The "rounding out" was completed in 1853, not by Buchanan, but by the U.S. diplomat James Gadsden, when he arranged a treaty with Mexico for the purchase of just over 29,000 square miles of desert south of Arizona's Gila River for ten million dollars. The United States bought the land in case it would be needed for the construction one day of a southern railroad out to California. The purchase was named in honor of the man who arranged it.[4]

The continental limits of the United States were now fully established. But another acquisition was to come fourteen years later—one far to the north of the forty-ninth parallel.

five

WILLIAM HENRY SEWARD AND HIS "ICE BOX"

•••

America's next great land acquisition was made in 1868. Purchased for the country were more than half a million acres of rugged land in the far northwestern region that would one day become the state of Alaska.

William Henry Seward

The man who negotiated the acquisition of Alaska and signed the treaty for its purchase was Secretary of State William Henry Seward. The fourth of six children, he was born in Florida, New York, in 1801, the very year that Madison became Jefferson's top cabinet officer. In one way, the two secretaries were much alike. Both were slightly built, with Seward, at five feet six inches, being just two inches taller than Madison. But there the similarity ended. Madison was deliberate in his thinking and personally shy, while the sociable Seward was quick, even impetuous, in his decisions.[1]

··· William H. Seward ···

Educated at Schenectady, New York, in his early years, Seward later studied law and was admitted to the bar in 1822. Then, finding himself attracted to the political life, he entered New York politics and began a career in which he served four years as a state senator, four as the state governor, and twelve as a U.S. senator. While still in the Senate, he ran for the Republican nomination in the 1860 presidential election, but lost to Abraham Lincoln.

The next year, the newly elected Lincoln named Seward as his secretary of state. At that time it was the custom for an incoming president to appoint a disappointed rival to the post. Lincoln chose Seward for this reason, but the selection proved a smart one. Seward had served on the Senate's foreign relations committee and was well versed in foreign affairs.

A year after Seward took office, the Civil War erupted and threatened to tear the nation apart. The conflict burdened him with many unexpected domestic and foreign responsibilities. At home, he was in charge of discovering southern sympathizers who were living in the north and could do damage to the federal cause. In international matters, he worked constantly to dissuade foreign countries from officially recognizing the Confederacy.

Seward employed the Monroe Doctrine to discourage foreign intervention on behalf of the South. Maintaining that his country was enmeshed in a domestic upheaval—not a war—he bluntly made it clear that any intervention would be viewed as an unfriendly act, a violation of the Doctrine. Taking him at his word, Britain, France, and other countries issued a proclamation of neutrality in the struggle.

Unfortunately, the fabric of the neutrality was flawed. The British, hoping to trade with the South if it won the war, sold six destroyers to the Confederacy. France's Napoleon the Third allowed the Confederacy to purchase destroyers from his shipyards and helped to arrange a loan for the South from a Paris bank. His motive in favoring the Confederacy was his desire to do something that his uncle—Napoleon Bonaparte —had failed to do early in the century—establish a French empire in the Americas. With the United States divided, he felt that his plan had a better chance of succeeding. In 1864, at the height of the Civil War, he placed Archduke Maxmillian of Austria on the Mexican throne.

Napoleon's foray into Mexico was a decided violation of the Monroe Doctrine. But the United States could do little more than send protest messages, as it did not wish to push France into recognizing the South. In the wake of the war, Seward persuaded Napoleon the Third to give up his Mexican empire. Napoleon withdrew his troops, Maxmillian was left behind to be executed by Mexican revolutionaries, and the strength of the Monroe Doctrine was confirmed.

On the night of April 14, 1865, just days after the Civil War ended, Seward was home asleep, recovering from injuries incurred in a traffic mishap, when a noise was heard in the hall outside his bedroom. His daughter Fanny, who was sitting at his bedside, opened the door to find her brother Fred arguing with a stranger. The stranger said that he had medicine for the secretary and must tell him how to take it. Fred refused him admittance, and Fanny returned to her father's bedside, closing the door behind her. The argument continued, and she asked the male nurse on duty in the bedroom to see what the matter was. When he went out to the hallway, the nurse was horrified to see a bloodied Fred lying in a heap and the stranger standing with a Bowie knife in hand. The stranger struck the nurse with the knife, dashed to Seward's bedside, and repeatedly slashed his face and neck. Fanny's screams brought other members of the household running and they wrestled the attacker out of the bedroom, only to have him break away and flee into the night.

At the same time as the attack, Abraham Lincoln was shot to death while watching a play at Ford's Theater. His killer was John Wilkes Booth, an actor with strong southern sympathies. Booth's action was part of a plot he had organized to assassinate Lincoln, Vice President Andrew Johnson, and Secretary Seward. Johnson was not attacked, and he assumed the presidency. Seward's assailant was found to be Lewis Powell (alias Lewis Payne), an ex-Confederate soldier who had lost two brothers in the war.

Only by the best of fortune and the quick action of his family did the secretary escape the tragedy that befell Lincoln. When Seward recovered from his injuries, he returned to his State Department duties. Now, as Andrew Johnson's top cabinet officer, he came to the high point of his career—the purchase of Alaska, an area that thousands of Americans were to nickname "Seward's Ice Box."

Seward and His Alaska "Ice Box"

As secretary of state, Seward was an ardent but peaceful expansionist.[2] He believed that America's greatness and safety depended much on the acquisition of areas outside the nation. In great part, his belief stemmed from his experiences in the Civil War, when he had seen how difficult it was for the navy to take on supplies in foreign ports. He was convinced that it was essential that the islands in the Atlantic, Caribbean, and Pacific be under the American flag for naval use in both war and peace and for safeguarding the nation's ocean commerce at all times.

As a peaceful expansionist, however, Seward did not believe in taking territories by force, so his term in office was marked by a series of attempted purchases. He vainly tried to buy Greenland and Iceland in the Atlantic and three Danish-owned islands in the Caribbean. He also explored the possibility of purchasing a string of other Caribbean islands, among them Puerto Rico and Cuba. Cuba, the largest of the Caribbean group, was his most coveted target for acquisition. In arguing on behalf of securing Cuba, the secretary voiced one quirky view that displayed a total ignorance of geological fact. He held that Cuba rightfully belonged to the United States because "every rock and every grain of sand in that island were drifted and washed out from American soil by the floods of the Mississippi, and other estuaries of the Gulf of Mexico."

(It was not until 1917 that the United States purchased holdings in the Caribbean. That year Secretary of State Robert Lansing arranged to buy from Denmark a group of some sixty-five small islands for twenty-five million dollars. Renamed the Virgin Islands of the United States and covering an area of 133 square miles at the edge of the Atlantic, they were bought to serve as a defensive line against foreign moves against the Caribbean and the Panama Canal.)

Looking to the Pacific, Seward cast his eye on Hawaii. He proposed a mutual-trade treaty with Hawaii that was meant to lead to the eventual annexation of the island chain. The idea got as far as a treaty, but it was rejected by Congress for fear that competition from Hawaii would damage the sugar and rice growers in the American South. The only ocean annexation that Seward was able to arrange was for Midway in the North Pacific.

The opportunity to make what proved to be his greatest acquisition—the Alaska territory—literally fell into his lap in the latter half of the 1860s. The vast land had been a Russian possession since the mid-1700s and was a region of both interest and concern for Americans. Their interest was piqued by the region's rich fur, whaling, and fishing resources. Triggering their concern was the knowledge that the Russians had moved down the Pacific coast some years ago and had established trading posts as far south as San Francisco Bay. Might not they expand even farther one day and cut the United States off from California, the state that the nation needed as a doorway to the Pacific Ocean?

Unknown to them, however, was the fact that Russia's Czar Alexander the Second had lost interest in holding Alaska. The region had always provided Russia with a rich trade in furs, but now—as the British had once felt about Oregon country—he believed that it had been "furred out" and was no longer of any real value to his country. Further, he felt that his nation was on the verge of war with its long-time enemy, Great Britain. He realized that, if war came, he would likely lose the defenseless Alaska to the British. Still further, he needed money to finance the anticipated conflict. The perfect solution to these problems: sell the frozen expanse to the Americans.

In 1867 the Czar's minister to Washington was instructed to open negotiations for the sale of the territory. An enthusiastic Seward represented the United States in the talks. Within a matter of weeks, a deal was struck and a treaty signed that, if approved by Congress, would see the territory pass into American hands for the sum of $7.2 million.

The news of the proposed treaty unleashed a storm of criticism throughout the country. Various newspapers declared that the United States already had enough territory and asked, "Why buy a Russian iceberg?" Other papers, among them Cincinnati's *Daily Gazette,* charged that the purchase was a tactic to divert attention from what they felt was President Johnson's and Secretary Seward's poor handling of domestic issues. Still others called the purchase a useless extravagance.

Most of the public agreed. Their annoyance at the purchase was possibly best revealed when the question of renaming the acquisition was discussed. The region had long been known as Russian America, a name now inappropriate. But what contributions did the public make to the discussion? From the public came such sarcastic entries as "Seward's Folly," "Seward's Ice Box," "Seward's Polar Bear Garden," and "Walrussia."

A minority of Americans supported the purchase. They felt that the new territory would serve the United States as a valuable naval base, would provide harbors for fishing and whaling fleets, and would enrich the nation with its timber and the wealth of other natural resources that it was rumored to contain. When the question of a new name arose, they eased the sting that Seward felt at the sarcasm in the opposition's suggestions. They proposed "Seward Land" and "Seward Territory." The Secretary himself finally christened the land "Alaska." The name is derived from an Aleut Eskimo word meaning "mainland."

In the face of a heated public opposition, Congress approved the acquisition. In great part, the national legislators recalled that Russia had been openly supportive of the federal government in the Civil War and now wanted to do the Czar a favor. Also, there were those rumored natural resources. If they were more than rumor, they would eventually prove immensely profitable for the nation.

The Alaska purchase was the ultimate victory for Seward in his quest for additional territories. As some Americans had envisioned, it proved to be a profitable victory. The Alaskan fishing and sealing trade yielded millions of dollars annually. In 1873 the territory that was to become the nation's forty-ninth state was found to be rich in gold. Subsequent years revealed it to contain oil, gas, coal, copper, iron, silver, platinum, tin, and mercury deposits. In brief, Seward's purchase has returned to the United States—financially and culturally—a wealth countless times greater than the price paid for it.

JOHN M. HAY, CHINA, AND THE PANAMA CANAL

• • •

Thirty-three years passed between the end of the Civil War and the outbreak of the Spanish-American War in 1898. This new struggle brought two unexpected results. First, it gained a number of overseas possessions for the United States; the country had always been a presence on the international scene, but the new possessions marked its beginnings as a major world power. Second, the conflict led to the nation's construction of one of the world's premier waterways—the Panama Canal.

These results caused the secretary of state to perform two significant tasks in foreign affairs: he dealt with the world's relations with China, and he played a key role in paving the way for building the Panama Canal. He was John M. Hay.

John M. Hay

Born in Salem, Indiana, on October 8, 1838, John M. Hay was an attorney who, after attending Brown University, practiced law in Springfield, Illinois.[1] There he met and deeply impressed a fellow lawyer, Abraham Lincoln. So highly did Lincoln think of Hay's abilities that, on entering the White House in 1861, he took the twenty-three-year-old man with him as his assistant private secretary. Hay worked at Lincoln's side throughout the Civil War and then, following the president's assassination, held diplomatic posts in France, Austria, and Spain. An accomplished writer, he later joined John C. Nicolay, Lincoln's chief private secretary, in writing the book *Abraham Lincoln: A History.*

Hay was named secretary of state in 1898 by William McKinley. He was the second secretary to serve McKinley, replacing a man with a similar name—William R. Day—who resigned the position after just six months. At the time Hay accepted the post, the Spanish-American War had just ended and the United States was beginning peace negotiations with Spain.

The Spanish-American War

The Spanish-American War was a conflict that had been in the making throughout the 1800s because of Spain's unremittingly harsh and brutal rule of its Caribbean island holding, Cuba.[2] The Cuban people finally rebelled in 1895 and plunged into a savage struggle with their mother country. With the outbreak threatening the safety of the American planters and business people in Cuba, the U.S. battleship *Maine* was dispatched in early 1898 to protect them. One February night, as the ship rode at anchor in Havana harbor, an explosion tore it to pieces and took the lives of 260 crewmen. Infuriated, the American people, who admired Cuba's bid for freedom, blamed Spain for the tragedy and called for revenge. Actually, the cause of the explosion was never learned. Several theories were discussed, among them the possibility that the ship's boilers had accidentally exploded, but the American public believed only one— that the *Maine* had been sabotaged by the Spanish in an effort to drive the United States out of Cuba. The nationwide call for revenge reached such a fever pitch that, on April 21, 1898,

Congress declared war against the country. In support of the Cuban people, legislators accompanied the declaration with the promise that America would make no claim on their island and would return it to them when the fight was won.

The war lasted just 113 days—until August 12, 1898. In that brief span, U.S. troops invaded Cuba and defeated the Spanish; far across the Pacific, a combined American-Filipino force took the city of Manila as the first step toward wresting the entire island chain from Spain. Elsewhere in the Pacific, U.S. troops captured the Spanish-held island of Guam and went ashore on unclaimed Wake Island; at the same time, Congress annexed Hawaii. All three islands were thought to be needed as fueling stations for the fighting in the Pacific.

Negotiations for a peace treaty began within weeks of the Spanish defeat. The job of arranging the treaty fell first to Secretary William R. Day and then to his successor, John M. Hay. Hay, thanks to his forcefulness and his past experiences as a diplomat, proved to be an expert negotiator. He pressed for and got the Spanish to agree to an idea that they hated—the ceding of the valuable Philippine chain to the United States in exchange for a payment of twenty million dollars. He also got them to hand over the islands of Guam in the Pacific and Puerto Rico in the Caribbean. As had been promised by Congress, Cuba was returned to its people.

The treaty was a significant one for the United States. It removed Spain as a power in the Western Hemisphere. Guam and Wake Island (along with annexed Hawaii) promised to make excellent refueling stations for American ships in both peace and war. The Philippines gave the United States a series of islands that were well placed for the protection of the nation's Asian trade and also offered profitable natural resources.

(The Filipino people had long been restive under Spanish rule and were no happier with the American presence. They campaigned tirelessly through the years for independence. In 1934 the U.S. Congress enacted legislation that promised them their freedom by 1946, with the intervening years to be spent preparing them to govern themselves. During World War Two the

··· John M. Hay ···

islands were occupied by the Japanese, but independence was established in 1946.)

The peace treaty opened the way for the two works for which Hay is best remembered. The first took shape when he looked to the Philippines and the land that lay just beyond it—China.

Hay and the "Open Door" for China

Hay cast a worried eye on China.[3] The ancient nation was beset with problems that stemmed from its defeat in three wars waged between the mid- and late-1800s. Left enfeebled by their costs, it had fallen prey to a string of countries—Britain, France, Germany, Russia, and Japan—that descended on China and divided its commerce among themselves. Each established its own Chinese area—its "sphere of influence"—for trade with the outside world.

China's plight alarmed many Americans for several reasons. For one, U.S. exporters worried that the intruders might soon ban everyone else from participating in the Chinese trade; if so, the United States would certainly be damaged economically. For another, Americans feared that one of the countries might become so powerful in China that it would try to grab the newly acquired Philippine islands.

Acting on this growing alarm, Hay sent a letter to all the world's major nations in 1899. In it, he urged them to endorse what he called an *Open Door policy* in China. This meant that the intruder countries would be fair to all other nations—including, of course, the United States—by "opening the door" to China and allowing them to trade there on an equal basis.

Only Italy—which had no sphere of influence in China—supported the "Open Door" concept. Russia politely rejected it. Japan, Britain, France, and Germany promised their support—but only if the other countries did the same. These answers disappointed Hay. He knew that his policy was destined to be a weak one, because the world was without an international body to enforce it. Nor could the United States alone act as the enforcer without risking a war with whichever country chose to ignore the policy. Nevertheless, since all the nations but one had failed to reject it outright, Hay boldly announced that the policy had been accepted in general and was now in effect.

In 1900 an upheaval in China enabled Hay to strengthen the policy. Ever since the foreign intrusions had begun, they had been opposed by many of the Chinese people. Among the most zealous of the opponents were the members of the *Order of Literary Patriotic Harmonious Fists,* a secret society dedicated to driving all foreigners out of the country. The society was nicknamed "the Boxers" because, as part of its program, it promoted training in sports, chiefly boxing. By 1900, the Boxers had grown so powerful that the Chinese government had to surrender the running of the nation's foreign affairs to them. They immediately demanded that all ministers of the foreign powers leave the country.

When the ministers balked, the Boxers attacked and killed the German ambassador in the streets of Peking. All other foreign dignitaries and businesspeople fled to the British embassy and barricaded its buildings and grounds as best they could. The Boxers laid siege to the embassy for fifty-five days.

Hay played a major part in assembling an 18,000-man rescue force for the beleaguered British embassy. The force consisted of British, French, Russian, Japanese, and U.S. troops. The American contingent totaled 2,500 men. On arriving in China, the rescuers crushed the rebellion and ended the power of the Boxers.

With one crisis out of the way, Hay immediately faced another. Britain, France, Germany, Russia, and Japan were now eager for revenge, and Hay feared that they would no longer limit themselves to their spheres of influence. Rather, he suspected that they would carve up the country among themselves for greater profits. In 1901 he sent all the powers another letter in which he said that the Open Door policy would now also apply to the protection of China's lands from foreign avarice. He pledged that the United States would take no territory there—and then persuaded Britain, France, and Germany to join him. Their agreement led the remaining powers to follow suit. The Open Door policy was given the extra strength it needed to work.

The policy proved generally effective for three decades—until Japan invaded Manchuria in 1931 and then went to war against China in 1937 as part of its campaign to become the dominant power in Asia. The "door," however, managed to remain "open" until China won full independence in the wake of World War Two.

In all, the policy did much to bring economic and international stability to the Far East. But it was to take second place to the work that came next for Hay.

Hay and the Panama Canal

At the time the Spanish-American War erupted, the U.S. battleship *Oregon* lay anchored at Seattle, Washington.[4] When the ship was summoned to the fighting in Cuba, it had to sail some 13,000 miles to reach its destination—a trip that carried the ship all the way down the Pacific to the foot of South America and then back up the Atlantic to the Caribbean. The long voyage revived interest in a very old proposal—the construction of a canal across some point in Central America that would shorten sea journeys from the Pacific to the Atlantic.

The idea dated back to the 1600s, when the first Spanish explorers in Central America saw that an Atlantic-Pacific waterway would speed the shipment of the New World's riches home to Spain. In the 1800s, America and Britain became interested in the project and entered into the Bulwer-Clayton Treaty, in which they agreed to build the canal together one day. They also agreed that it could be laid out along either of two routes—one across Nicaragua, the other across the Isthmus of Panama.

While Britain and the United States talked, the French took action. Their most famous engineer, Ferdinand de Lesseps, who had headed construction of the Suez Canal, began digging a path across the Isthmus of Panama, the narrowest stretch of land in Central America. His effort met with failure, and France was forced to abandon the project in 1889.

In 1901, when President McKinley was assassinated, Vice President Theodore Roosevelt moved into the White House. He had long believed that America should take on the job of constructing the canal, which would be of great military benefit to the nation in wartime. In peacetime it would serve as a splendid trade route not only for America but for countries everywhere. At his urging, Congress passed an authorization to build the canal.

Roosevelt chose Panama as the location for the waterway. But before construction could begin, a number of obstacles had to be surmounted. The new chief executive asked Hay to remain as secretary and charged him with the task of clearing these obstacles. First, Hay arranged for cancellation of the old Bulwer-Clayton Treaty so that the United States could construct the Panama Canal on its own, without Britain. In 1901 he and Julian Pauncefote, the British ambassador in Washington, negotiated a pact that became known as the Hay-Pauncefote Treaty, in which Britain agreed to let the United States carry out the construction by itself. For its part, America promised to keep the future passageway open to all nations during times of peace and to charge an equal fee to all ships sailing through it.

Hay now turned to his next task—a string of negotiations with Colombia, whose permission was required before any digging could begin in its province. Hay's talks with the Columbian government ended happily in 1903 with the Hay-Herran Treaty. Granted to the United States was a strip of land six miles wide, along which the canal was to run; the strip followed the general route that de Lesseps had chosen. In return, the United States was to pay Colombia ten million dollars for the land and an annual fee of $250,000 once the canal was open.

The treaty had to be approved by both the American and Colombian congresses. The U.S. Congress quickly gave its blessing, but Roosevelt and Hay were stunned when the Colombian Congress rejected the pact and demanded that the United States pay more—fifteen million dollars—for the digging rights.

The Panamanian people had long chafed under Colombian rule and had fought five times in the 1800s to free themselves. They looked on the proposed canal as a boon that would bring them widespread employment and, on hearing of the fate of the Hay-Herran agreement, they exploded in fury and prepared to rebel against Colombia.

Roosevelt, seeing the advantage to the United States in the potential revolt, quickly sided with the Panamanians. When Colombia sent 500 men to quiet the upheaval, he ordered a gunboat to Panama that prevented the troops from landing. The Panamanians then staged a month-long bloodless revolution that made their country an independent nation.

That month, Hay and Panamanian representative Philippe Bunau-Varilla negotiated Panama's permission to build the canal and signed the Hay-Bunau-Varilla Treaty. The terms of the agreement were essentially the same as in the Hay-Herran Treaty. For a payment of ten million dollars and an annual fee of $250,000, America was granted a strip of land across the isthmus for the canal's construction and future operation. There was only one change: the strip was extended to a ten-mile width.

The treaty was signed on November 18, 1903, and approved by Congress in early 1904. The way was at last opened for the building of the waterway that, when completed in 1914, would be called one of the engineering wonders of the world—a title that it holds to this day.

...

As America emerged as a major world power, John Hay displayed an understanding of international problems that was essential for the nation's future. In his Open Door policy, he recognized that a stable Asia was necessary for the benefit of traders and investors everywhere. His Panama Canal work revealed a far-reaching vision not only of America's future trading needs as a major power but of the entire world's.

CHARLES EVANS HUGHES AND THE QUEST FOR PEACE

• • •

For more than a century after the Monroe Doctrine was formulated, the United States kept its promise not to engage in the wars of foreign nations (the exception being the Boxer rebellion). When World War One erupted in Europe in 1914, the country at first refused to take sides. But then, in 1915, it began to turn away from the doctrine. That year, a German U-boat torpedoed and sank the liner *Lusitania* at the cost of more than 100 American lives. The nation was enraged and ready to declare war on Germany, because the U-boat had violated a basic law of the sea—warships could not sink merchant and passenger vessels without prior warning and without insuring the safety of the people aboard.

But the United States held its temper until 1917, when further German sea attacks drove it to fight alongside the Allied nations (a coalition of states headed by the British Empire, France, and Russia). America's participation in the conflict lasted for little more than a year before an armistice ended the fighting on November 11, 1918.

A few months later, representatives of the Allied nations and Germany met in France and worked out terms of the Treaty of Versailles, which formally ended the war. The treaty had to be ratified by the legislatures of the participating countries, and, to the world's surprise, the U.S. Congress refused to give the pact its blessing.

Why? The treaty was based on fourteen points that President Woodrow Wilson had developed in the hope of ending war for all time.[1] The points included the banning of secret treaties that had often led to war in the past; the guarantee that the ships of neutral nations would be safe at sea during wartime; and the alteration of certain national boundaries to end the border disputes that had caused friction in Europe over the years. With one exception, Wilson's fourteen points enjoyed wide support in the United States. That single exception was a provision within the fourteenth one. The fourteenth point itself was applauded by many Americans because it called for the formation of an organization of countries—the League of Nations—that would promote global peace. But it contained a provision that required the member nations to fight on behalf of any fellow member whose political independence was threatened by an aggressor nation.

Congressmen reacted angrily to the provision, saying that it would cause the United States to be dragged helplessly into other peoples' wars. The legislators flatly refused to sign the Treaty of Versailles. As a result, the United States remained outside the League of Nations, which had a membership of sixty-three countries, and remained without an official peace agreement with Germany for another two years.

Charles Evans Hughes

The son of a Baptist minister, Hughes was born in Glenn Falls, New York, on April 11, 1862.[2] He was a precocious child who learned to read at age three and was poring over the Bible, doing arithmetic problems, and studying Latin and German by the time he was six. He completed high school at thirteen and

··· Charles Evans Hughes and wife ···

Brown University at nineteen. Earning his law degree at the Columbia Law School, he passed the New York State bar examination with the highest grade given up to that time—99$^1/_2$ percent.

Hughes grew into a solitary man who had no special friends or confidants (President Theodore Roosevelt described him as "the bearded iceberg"). But, though he presented an aloof, cold, and austere exterior, Hughes was a caring husband and the loving father of three children.

A man who drove himself mercilessly at his work, Hughes carved out a remarkable career in public service. He spent three years as the governor of New York and then, in 1910, was appointed to the U.S. Supreme Court as an associate justice. In 1916, he resigned from the Court to wage an unsuccessful campaign for the presidency, and in 1921 newly elected President Warren G. Harding named him secretary of state.

Hughes and the Quest for World Peace

At the time Hughes became secretary, the country faced a major piece of unfinished business.[3] Since it had not signed the Treaty of Versailles, the United States had yet to make a formal peace with Germany. The new secretary immediately traveled to the former enemy country and arranged the Treaty of Berlin. In general, the terms of the pact were the same as those in the Treaty of Versailles, including the point calling for the establishment of the League of Nations. Left out, however, was the provision that would have enabled the League to send the United States to war.

Congress ratified the Berlin agreement on Hughes's return. Though now free to join the League, the United States never sought membership. The reason? Great segments of the public and many of the nation's leaders held strong isolationist views in the 1920s. Suffering from the memory of the country's losses in World War One, they wanted no part of dangerous foreign entanglements. Two oceans separated the country from nations whose hatreds of one another had so often ended in warfare. The desire to be left alone prevailed among many Americans throughout the 1930s—right up to the day the country was plunged into World War Two.

The Washington Disarmament Conference

Though refusing to join the League, the nation was eager for peace and wanted to reduce the amount of money that it was still spending for defense. To prevent another war, Harding charged his Secretary of State with a new task—an international conference to reduce the arms held by the world's nations.

Hughes invited countries everywhere to send delegates to a series of meetings at Washington, D.C. Eight nations accepted the invitation—Belgium, Britain, China, France, Italy, Japan, Holland, and Portugal.

Their delegates arrived in the U.S. capital in November 1921 and worked together until the following February. They discussed the limitation of land and naval armaments and the rules for governing the use of new military weapons, such as poison gas, which had been unleashed in World War One and had harmed thousands of men on both sides.

The United States was particularly interested in reducing its costly building program for the navy. But Hughes was aware of Britain's superior fleet and of the fact that Japan was rapidly strengthening its naval muscle. Back in 1902, the British and the Japanese had entered a pact in which they promised to assist each other in the event of war. The secretary feared that, should his country ever be forced to fight one, it would have to take on the other as well. To avoid this, he gambled on a daring step. In his opening address to the conference, he stunned the delegates by challenging them to join the United States in a sweeping reduction of their fleets.

He stated the number of battleships that America was ready to destroy. His frank statement, along with the intimation that other nations could do no less, charmed the U.S. public and people across the world. Some delegates, however, anything but charmed, balked at following Hughes's lead. In the end, he convinced four countries—Britain, France, Italy, and Japan—to join him. A British officer remarked humorously that the secretary, in his opening speech, sank "more ships in fifteen minutes than all the admirals of the world have sunk in a cycle of centuries."

The Washington conference ended with the United States, Britain, France, Italy, and Japan signing the Five Power Treaty. It limited the tonnage of their naval fleets: Britain and the United States were allowed 500,000 tons each; Japan was permitted 315,000 tons; and France and Italy were restricted to 175,000 tons each. These limitations required the United States to scrap thirty battleships and abandon two of four under construction at the time. Great Britain was allowed to complete two new ships. Japan had to get rid of one battleship. Finally, the treaty exacted a pledge from the five nations not to build any warships for a period of ten years.

In addition, the conference resulted in two other treaties:

The Four-Power Treaty: In this pact, the United States, Britain, Japan, and China each agreed to respect the other's possessions and to advise one another if a dispute developed regarding any of the holdings. They also agreed to stop fortifying their possessions. Finally, to Hughes's great relief, the treaty scrapped the Anglo-Japanese pact of 1902.

The Nine-Power Treaty: Signed by all the nations in attendance, this agreement reiterated and supported the terms of the Open Door policy.

The American people—in fact, the people of the entire world—greeted the three pacts with great relief and enthusiasm. The trio promised a permanent basis for world peace by generating international goodwill and eliminating the dangerous growth of battle fleets. In American eyes, Hughes was a true hero—the greatest secretary of state in a century.

Sadly, the peace that Hughes sought did not last. Japan, in its conquest to become the dominant power in Asia, attacked

Manchuria and China in the 1930s and fortified its Pacific holdings; the United States, though knowing that Japan was breaking the treaties, did not belong to the League of Nations and could not direct the League to curb Japan's actions. Nor could the United States use the League to speak out against the terrible threat to peace posed by the Hitler regime in Germany.

Still, Hughes was to go down in American history as among the finest of the nation's secretaries of state. He served under Harding until 1925 and then briefly under President Calvin Coolidge. He resigned to return to private law practice, but in 1930 he was named Chief Justice of the United States Supreme Court, a post he held until his retirement in 1941.

Though Hughes came to the State Department with scant experience in foreign affairs, he possessed other assets: superb intelliegence, integrity, the ability to work hard, and the knack for surrounding himself with excellent career diplomats. Unfortunately, the peace that Hughes and the world so desired in the early twentieth century was to be trampled under the hobnail boots of Adolf Hitler's armies in the late 1930s.

eight

EDWARD R. STETTINIUS AND THE UNITED NATIONS

• • •

Throughout the 1930s, as Japan extended its power in Asia and Germany's Adolf Hitler sent a mounting wave of fear through Europe, the United States remained an isolationist country, loathe to become enmeshed in foreign quarrels. When World War Two erupted in Europe in 1939, America steered clear of the fighting, though it provided needed military equipment to Britain, China, and others of the Allied nations. Finally, when the Japanese attacked Pearl Harbor in December 1941, the country entered conflict.

Representatives of the major Allied nations met throughout the war to coordinate their fighting efforts. In 1941, at a meeting in Washington, D.C., the representatives of twenty-six nations used the name President Franklin D. Roosevelt had suggested, the "United Nations,"[1] when they signed a pledge to stand together until the war was won. They called the pact the United Nations Declaration.

In October 1943 the foreign ministers of the three largest Allied countries—the United States, Britain, and the Soviet Union—assembled in Moscow to discuss the course of the war and the postwar future. Representing the United States at the session was Roosevelt's secretary of state, Cordell Hull. The trio agreed to establish at the earliest possible date an international organization for ensuring world peace. The new organization, known as the United Nations, would replace the League of Nations, which had been helpless to stop the aggressions that led to World War Two.

Later in the year, the chiefs of state of the "big three" nations—America's Roosevelt, British Prime Minister Winston Churchill, and Soviet Premier Joseph Stalin—gathered at Teheran, Persia, for the first of their wartime meetings. There they planned the defeat of the enemy powers, and, looking to a time beyond the war, issued an invitation to all countries to join "a family of democratic nations" that would be dedicated to world peace and security. The invitation paved the way for further development of the United Nations organization.

The first of that work was done in 1944, when representatives of the United States, Britain, the Soviet Union, and China assembled for a meeting at the Dumbarton Oaks estate near Washington, D.C. The purpose of the Dumbarton Oaks Conference was to develop proposals for the creation of the United Nations. Hosting the conference was America's new secretary of state, Edward R. Stettinius, Jr., who had just replaced Cordell Hull.

Edward R. Stettinius

Born in Chicago on October 22, 1900, Stettinius, the son of well-to-do parents,[2] grew into a hardworking, genial man with deep sympathy for people less privileged than he. He demonstrated that sympathy when, while attending the University of Virginia, he showed a greater interest in helping the poor families of Albermarle County than in achieving high grades. He ended up not taking a degree from the school.

That sympathy was again evident when, at age twenty-six, Stettinius became an assistant to John L. Pratt, vice president at General Motors Corporation. As Pratt's assistant in charge of employee welfare matters, he negotiated one of the country's earliest group health insurance programs for company workers. He went on to become General Motors' vice president in charge of industrial and public relations.

Stettinius moved to the United States Steel Corporation in 1933 and, five years later, when he was just thirty-eight years old, became chairman of the company's board of directors. In that capacity he successfully fought off a board move to lower employee salaries when, because of the Depression, the price that the company was able to charge for its steel dropped. His stand caught the eye of President Roosevelt. The president praised U.S. Steel for its "statesmanship" in protecting employee salaries and, liking what Stettinius did, called him to government service.

Between 1941 and 1943, Stettinius worked on America's Lend-Lease program. Enacted in 1941 by Congress, the program authorized the government to transfer, lend, or lease "any defense article" to "the government of any country whose defense the President deems vital to the defense of the United States." During the war years, the United States provided Britain, the Soviet Union, China, and other Allied nations with more than fifty billion dollars in military equipment and services.

In 1943 Stettinius was appointed under secretary of state and a year later, on Secretary of State Cordell Hull's departure from office, he was named to head the State Department.

Stettinius and the United Nations

One of the new secretary's first tasks was to host the Dumbarton Oaks Conference.[3] Between August and October of 1944, he and the delegates from Britain, the Soviet Union, and China worked out a basic framework for the future United Nations. The results of their work became known as the Dumbarton Oaks Proposals.

··· Edward R. Stettinius (left) and
President Franklin Delano Roosevelt ···

The Dumbarton Oaks Proposals

On reviewing the proposals, President Roosevelt and Stettinius
both remembered the fate of the League of Nations in the United
States. They considered the country's refusal to join the league
to be a major mistake and wanted to make sure that the error
was not repeated. They launched under Stettinius's leadership

an information campaign about the United Nations that inundated Americans with everything from booklets, comic books, and cartoons to radio addresses and public speeches by government officials. The campaign also distributed millions of copies of the Dumbarton Oaks Proposals.

Four months after the Dumbarton Oaks Conference ended, Roosevelt met with Churchill and Stalin for the final time in World War Two. At the meeting, which was held in February 1945 at the resort city of Yalta on Russia's Crimean peninsula, the three leaders laid the plans for Hitler's final defeat in Europe, and they also discussed the soon-to-be-born United Nations.

Stettinius, who accompanied Roosevelt to the meeting, clarified a number of points in the Dumbarton Oaks Proposals for Churchill and Stalin. At the close of the meeting, the three leaders called for an international conference to form the United Nations, scheduled to begin on April 25, 1945, in San Francisco, California.

The San Francisco Conference

Roosevelt gave Stettinius the job of preparing for the historic meeting and leading the American delegation. But the president, whose health had been shattered by the stresses of his wartime leadership, did not live to see his secretary depart for San Francisco. He died suddenly of a cerebral hemorrhage on April 12, just two weeks before the conference was to open and less than a month before Hitler's final defeat in Germany. Vice President Harry S. Truman entered the White House.

Truman, knowing of the work that Stettinius was doing to breathe life into the United Nations, asked him to remain as secretary of state and to proceed with plans for the conference. On a rainy April 25, 1945, 200 representatives from forty-six nations assembled in San Francisco for the meeting's opening ceremonies.

Forming the basis for the San Francisco discussions were the Dumbarton Oaks Proposals. Out of those proposals came

··· (Left to right) V. M. Molotov *(U.S.S.R.)*, E.R. Stettinius ···
(U.S.A.), and Anthony Eden *(U.K.)* at the
San Franciso Conference in 1945.

the United Nations Charter. It called for a world organization that
would consist of six departments:

> *The General Assembly:* Made up of all the member
> nations, it would serve as a forum to air international
> problems and opinions.

The Security Council: On the shoulders of the council would rest the responsibility for maintaining global peace and security. It would consist of eleven nations, five of whom—Britain, China, France, the Soviet Union, and the United States—were to be permanent members, with six others to serve two-year terms. (Since then, the council's membership had been boosted to fifteen, with the original five countries still serving permanently.)

The International Court of Justice: It would resolve legal disputes among the member nations.

The Economic and Social Council: It would promote higher living standards, full employment, and economic and social improvements for the member nations.

The Trusteeship Council: It would help subjugated peoples move toward self-government or independence.

The Secretariat: It would act as secretary to all the U.N. departments. Its work would include preparing the agenda for meetings, collecting information, registering treaties, and publishing documents and reports.

On June 26, 1945, the delegates of forty-nine nations (three had joined the original forty-six since the start of the conference) signed the charter, with a fourth nation, Poland, adding its signature in mid-October. Stettinius signed the document on behalf of the United States.

Before the United Nations could begin work, the charter had to be ratified by a majority of the legislatures of the signatory nations. The necessary ratifications were made by October 24, the day on which the world organization became a reality. In the United States, the Senate—in marked contrast to the treatment given to the League of Nations a quarter-century earlier—approved the charter by a vote of eighty-nine to two. World War Two and the nation's responsibilities in its wake had taught America that it was no longer possible to be an isolationist country.

The day after the San Francisco conference was adjourned, Stettinius submitted his resignation as secretary. The secretary of state, on Roosevelt's death, had moved a step closer in the line of presidential succession. Stettinius knew that Truman felt that any successor to the presidency should "have held at least some office to which he had been elected by a vote of the people," and Stettinius had never held an elected position.

Truman, however, did not release Stettinius from all public service. In the fall of 1945 he sent the former secretary to London as chairman of the U.S. delegation to the United Nations' Preparatory Commission meeting. The purpose of the session was to formulate the rules for how the organization would conduct its business.

In January, 1946 Stettinius served as a member of the American delegation to the first session of the U.N.'s General Assembly at Paris. He went on to represent the United States on the Security Council, serving until 1946, when he resigned from government service. He lived until 1949.

On his death, Stettinius was remembered with deep respect by the U.N.'s secretary-general, Trygve Lie of Norway. The secretary-general said that the former secretary of state "will live in history as one of the chief architects of the United Nations."

In the years since its organization, the United Nations has grown to a membership of 184 countries. It performs valuable work for the entire world—in peacekeeping, health, the welfare of children, the eradication of illiteracy, and the settlement of international problems. But, less than two years after its birth in 1945, the organization saw its ideals shaken to the core when two of its founding nations—the United States and the Soviet Union—embarked on the "Cold War." The struggle rocked the world and shaped America's foreign policy for years to come.

n i n e

GEORGE C. MARSHALL AND A NEW "WAR"
•••

No sooner had World War Two ended than a new war erupted. It was a political and ideological struggle that was fought by the Soviet Union and the world's Communist countries on one side, and the United States and its fellow democracies on the other. Quickly christened the "Cold War" by the press, it raged for four decades before ending at the dawn of the 1990s. Though the Cold War dates from the mid-1940s, its origins can be traced to 1917 and World War One. In that year, battered by the fighting and their longtime miserable living conditions, the Russian people rose up and overthrew their despotic tsarist government. Established in its place was a government headed by the Bolsheviks—the Communist Party.

Throughout those decades, the Americans viewed the growth of communism worldwide with alarm. They put their alarm aside during World War Two (though they remained suspicious of communist ambitions) to fight alongside the Soviets against Hitler. But it returned at war's end when Soviet premier Joseph Stalin began bringing a number of European countries—among them Czechoslovakia, Hungary, Poland, and

··· General George C. Marshall ···

Romania—under his control. Stalin claimed that these takeovers were made solely for the defense of his country. Because the Soviet Union had been invaded from the west by Germany in 1941, he said he wanted to guard his frontiers with satellite nations that would make another invasion from the west too difficult to risk.

The United States opposed Stalin's actions on two counts. First, detesting his communist dictatorship, it wanted to safeguard other peoples against his ambitions. Second, the United States was certain that Stalin was not simply trying to protect his country against some future invasion, but to extend his grip to areas beyond eastern Europe. The truth of this could be seen in Communist upheavals in Greece, France, and defeated Germany itself. At war's end, the conquered nation had been divided into four sectors, with the four Allied nations—Britain, France, Russia, and the United States—each given a sector to control. Stalin was rapidly turning the Russian sector into a Communist state.

All these actions—plus the rise of communism in China—were enough to cause tension between America and Russia. But the tension heightened when the United States decided to take steps to slow down or stop Stalin's ambitions. Serving as secretary of state at the time was George C. Marshall.

George C. Marshall

Born at Uniontown, Pennsylvania, on December 31, 1880, George Catlett Marshall was the first career soldier ever to be named secretary of state.[1] Though he dreamed of joining the army throughout his childhood, he gave scant indication in his early schooling of the splendid military career that was to be his. He showed little interest in "book learning" and earned only fair grades. Later, he applied himself to his studies at the Virginia Military Institute and was voted senior first captain of the corps by his classmates. It was the highest cadet rank at the school. In his senior year, he went out for football, won a line position, and played so well that he was named to the all-southern team. He graduated fifteenth in his class in 1901 and was commissioned a second lieutenant.

As a young officer in World War One, Marshall saw battle service in France. His abilities were early recognized by General John ("Blackjack") Pershing, the commander of the U.S. forces in Europe, and he served in the postwar years as an aide to the general. Rising through the ranks, he was named assistant chief of staff of the Army in July 1938, deputy chief of staff the following October, and finally Chief of Staff the next year.

As chief of staff in World War Two, Marshall headed America's military forces and served as President Franklin D. Roosevelt's principal military adviser. Under his wartime leadership, the armed forces grew to more than eight million men and women. The nation's air force increased its strength to some 69,000 aircraft of all types. The leading military figures in the war—among them General Dwight D. Eisenhower and the Air Force's General Henry ("Hap") Arnold—were named to their commands by Marshall.

At age sixty-five, he retired from military service in November 1945, after both the European and Japanese wars had been won. But his retirement lasted no longer than a week. President Harry S. Truman asked him to go to China to help end a civil war there between the nation's nationalist and communist factions. He consented to the trip, only to have it meet with failure in the face of stubborn resistance by both sides.

In January 1947, Truman appointed Marshall secretary of state, a job that the retired general did not want but accepted out of a sense of duty to his country. Marshall, whom the president admired deeply and looked on as a loyal friend, was Truman's third secretary of state. He entered the State Department in the wake of Edward Stettinius, who resigned in 1945 after seeing the United Nations established, and James Byrnes, who worked until 1947 and then retired due to poor health. As soon as he took the post, Marshall found himself facing the problems of the Cold War and the task of formulating a U.S. policy that would deter the growing global threat of communism.

Marshall and the Truman Doctrine

In a 100,000-word State Department document on Soviet-American relations, Truman, Marshall, Dean Acheson (the under secretary of state and Marshall's chief aide), and other key government figures developed the policy.[2] The document, which was based on reports from U.S. representatives the world over, held that Stalin sought global domination and that Communism's armed forces in Europe and Asia now outnumbered those of the United States and its fellow democracies. Short of another world war, there was only one way to stop him. America had to adopt a policy of "containment," which would resist communist aggressions wherever they loomed in the world, with financial aid to the nations threatened by those aggressions, and with military help if needed.

Truman had to present the policy to Congress for approval, and the State Department was given the job of preparing the speech that the president would deliver to the legislators. The first beneficiaries of the proposed policy were to be Greece and Turkey. A communist-backed revolution in Greece seemed just weeks away from causing the nation's government to topple. Stalin was demanding that Turkey let him share in the control of the Dardanelles Strait. Control there would give him a trade and military river passage from southern Russia to the Mediterranean. If both Greece and Turkey fell to him and his power was extended to the Mediterranean, he could then move into the oil-rich Middle East.

Both the policy and an appeal for help for Greece and Turkey were worked into the speech that Truman delivered to Congress in March 1947. In the speech, which lasted just eighteen minutes, the president said:

> At the present moment in world history nearly every nation must choose between alternative ways of life. The choice too often is not to be a free one.
>
> One way of life is based upon the will of the majority, and is distinguished by free institutions, representa-

tive government, free elections, guarantees of individual liberty, freedom of speech and religion, and freedom from oppression.

The second way of life is based upon the will of a minority forcibly imposed upon the majority. It relies upon oppression, a controlled press and radio, fixed elections, and the suppression of personal freedoms.

I believe that it must be the policy of the United States to support free peoples who are resisting attempted subjugation by armed minorities or by outside pressures.

I believe we must assist free peoples to work out their own destinies in their own way.

I believe that our help should be primarily through economic and financial aid which is essential to economic and orderly political process.

With those few words, the president outlined what became known as the Truman Doctrine. Like the Monroe Doctrine of more than a century earlier, it became the cornerstone of America's foreign policy for years to come.

Truman then asked Congress to launch the policy of containment by authorizing $300 million for Greece and $100 million for Turkey to bolster their economic and military strength. The policy and the funds were approved, with the money contributing much to helping the two countries remain free of Stalin's grasp.

The Truman Doctrine was the first American salvo fired in the Cold War. The second was fired by Marshall himself.

Marshall and a Torn Europe

Europe lay in ruins at the close of World War Two.[3] Entire cities had been leveled. Several hundred million people were on the streets—divided between those whose homes had been ripped apart by bombing raids and artillery attacks and those who had survived the Nazi slave labor camps or gas chambers. Starvation was everywhere.

Secretary Marshall saw the situation as not only tragic but as a threat to the freedoms of the torn countries as well. With their people homeless and starving, they were prime targets for takeovers by communist factions that promised them better lives. The secretary knew that something must be done to offset this threat.

The idea of how to solve the problem began to take shape when he and his fellow delegates were flying home from Moscow after attending an international conference on the future of Germany. While talking about the Communist threat to the western European nations, they agreed that the United States should help strengthen them economically so that they could repel the threat, as it was doing for Greece and Turkey with the Truman Doctrine.

Some weeks later, after numerous talks with staff members and foreign affairs experts, Marshall assembled their ideas and put them into a speech that he delivered on June 5, 1947, during commencement exercises at Harvard University. In that speech, he introduced what became known as the European Recovery Program, or, as it was soon popularly called, the Marshall Plan.

His listeners heard him call on the European countries to get together and decide what they could do to help themselves recover and then tell the United States what additional financial aid they needed for the task. If they would do that and also pledge that any U.S. aid would be used for the economic benefit of all Europe, the United States would be willing to assist them.

The plan was enthusiastically welcomed in Europe. In September 1947, sixteen nations gathered in Paris to discuss a unified program of reconstruction. Not present were Russia and its satellite states; Stalin readily saw the dangers in the Marshall Plan to the spread of his power. Out of the meeting came the desired unified program.

The program called for spending nearly twenty-two billion dollars over a four-year period. Some of the money would be provided by the nations themselves and by the International Bank for Reconstruction and Development. But most—some seventeen billion dollars—would be supplied by the United States.

The United States lived up to Marshall's promise in 1948 when Congress passed the Economic Co-Operation Act, which authorized 5.3 billion dollars for the plan during its first year. Four years later the nation had loaned or given over twelve billion dollars to assist the European nations. The money was well spent. The plan helped many countries improve their industrial output by 7 to 9 percent annually. Farmers of western Europe claimed the highest rate of production in their history. The standard of living steadily improved throughout the war-ravaged continent.

For his part in devising the European Recovery Program, Secretary Marshall was awarded the Nobel Peace Prize in 1953. He became the fourth of only five secretaries to be honored with the prestigious award to date; the others are Elihu Root, Frank Kellogg, Cordell Hull, and Henry Kissinger.

Marshall fell ill soon after his plan was adopted and resigned as secretary in 1949. He returned to government service a year later as secretary of defense during the Korean War and retired permanently in 1951. He lived until 1959.

··· Dean Acheson ···

FOUR SECRETARIES AND THE COLD WAR
•••

Twelve men served as secretary during the years of the Cold War. Here are the stories of four of the best known of their number—Dean Acheson, John Foster Dulles, Dean Rusk, and Henry Kissinger.

Dean Acheson and the Cold War

If ever there was a secretary of state who looked like a diplomat, it was Dean Acheson.[1] Standing over six feet tall, he was dignified in bearing and handsome with his bristly but neatly trimmed mustache.

Born in Middletown, Connecticut, on April 11, 1893, Acheson was educated at a private school and Harvard University, where he earned a law degree. In the 1920s and 1930s, he practiced law and served as secretary to two U.S. Supreme Court justices—Louis D. Brandeis and Felix Frankfurter. He joined the State Department in 1941 and became under secretary of state in 1945 at the start of Harry S. Truman's presidency. Acheson first served under Secretary James Byrnes and then remained at his post when George C. Marshall took over from Byrnes in 1947.

While working under Marshall, Acheson helped to formulate the Truman Doctrine and the Marshall Plan. Truman rewarded him by promoting him to the top cabinet post on the general's resignation in 1949. It was a year that marked a changing attitude toward the Truman Doctrine.

The doctrine had always depended on financial aid to curb the spread of Communism. But now it was believed that such aid was not enough to halt Stalin. Armed muscle and the resolve to use it were also needed. This belief led Acheson to one of his most significant Cold War tasks.

For several years, the free nations of Europe had been discussing the possibility of an alliance to defend themselves against Soviet aggression. Immediately on his promotion, Acheson carried out a series of negotiations that, within a few months, turned the alliance into a reality. At mid-year, twelve nations signed a pact that created the North Atlantic Treaty Organization (NATO). The twelve—Belgium, Canada, Denmark, France, Great Britain, Iceland, Italy, Luxembourg, the Netherlands, Norway, Portugal, and the United States—pledged to keep the peace among themselves and to give military and economic aid to one another. Most important of all, with the ambitious Stalin in mind, they agreed to regard an attack against any one of them as an attack against them all.

Later joined by four other countries—Greece, Turkey, the Federal Republic of Germany, and Spain—NATO and its armed forces served as a deterrent to Soviet aggression in Europe for four decades—until the collapse of the Soviet Union in the late 1980s.

Acheson's next important Cold War work came in 1950, when North Korean Communist forces attacked South Korea. Truman immediately called in the secretary and other cabinet members to discuss what action the United States should take in response to this latest aggression. The president decided to commit troops to Korea to drive the invaders out. Acheson followed up on the decision by convincing America's fellow democracies and the United Nations to support the U.S. action. In the end, the North Koreans were faced not only by American troops but by a combined United Nations force.

In the next years, Acheson pushed for the expansion of NATO and the rearmament of West Germany as defensive measures for Europe. In 1951, along with delegates from forty-eight nations, he signed the 1951 peace treaty that formally ended the war with Japan. At the same time, he put his signature to a U.S. defense pact with Japan. In these and other works, he was always attempting to strengthen the Truman Doctrine.

Acheson left the State Department in 1953, when Dwight D. Eisenhower assumed the presidency. Replaced by John Foster Dulles, he practiced law and, until his death in 1971, gave much of his time to advising succeeding presidents, among them Lyndon B. Johnson and John F. Kennedy.

John Foster Dulles and the Cold War

John Foster Dulles was born in Washington, D.C., on February 25, 1888.[2] He was the descendant of two former secretaries of state. His grandfather, John W. Foster, was appointed by Benjamin Harrison. His uncle, Robert Lansing, served under Woodrow Wilson. As a young man, Dulles burned with the ambition to achieve the office himself. This ambition was realized when President Eisenhower called for him in 1953.

Dulles attended Princeton University and the Washington University School of Law, graduating from both with high honors and entering public service soon after. In his first job, he provided legal advice for the U.S. delegation at the Versailles Peace Conference that brought World War One to a formal end. Years later, in 1950, he undertook another peace mission, this one stemming from the fact that Allied nations had yet to mark the end of World War Two by signing a peace treaty with Japan. Dulles was appointed as a special U.S. ambassador to work out the long-overdue pact.

The assignment sent him on a 125,000-mile journey to visit the countries that had fought in the Pacific war—Australia, New Zealand, the Philippines, and Britain—and to fashion a treaty that would be acceptable to all. The task was a difficult one because many of the Allies, remembering the cruelty of some Japanese soldiers during the fighting, wanted a pact that would severely punish Japan. America, however, sought a gentler pact because it wanted to have the former enemy join the anti-Communist free nations.

Despite the difficulties he faced, Dulles negotiated a pact that was acceptable to everyone concerned. A number of other diplomats played a role in formulating the treaty, but all agreed that it was Dulles's skill in handling the various nations that made it possible. The treaty, which was signed by Secretary Acheson in 1951, is still considered a brilliant diplomatic triumph.

Along with his negotiating skill, Dulles showed himself to be a very tough-minded Cold War leader when he became secretary of state. His term in office was marked by a major Cold War success, a partial success, and an outright failure.

A Success: Halting the Korean War

No sooner had he been appointed secretary than Dulles showed his tough-mindedness in his efforts to end the Korean War. Since 1950 the war had seesawed back and forth between the opponents—the United States and the United Nations on one side and the North Koreans assisted by Red Chinese troops and supported by the Soviet Union on the other—with the American public growing increasingly tired of a conflict that was obviously going nowhere. General Eisenhower won the 1952 presidential election in great part by promising to bring the fighting to an end.

Eisenhower kept his promise after he won the White House. He and Dulles immediately sent a blunt message to China. In it they warned that, if the conflict did not end immediately, U.N. forces would begin bombing Chinese supply lines. There was little doubt that the two men intended to use nuclear

··· Attending the Council of Foreign Ministers Meeting ···
in 1949 were (left to right) Philip C. Jessup, Dean Acheson,
John Foster Dulles, and W. Averell Harriman.

weapons for the job, even at the risk of triggering a larger war.
The prospect of nuclear warfare terrified the world.

But the Eisenhower-Dulles warning worked. A truce was
signed between the warring parties on July 27, 1953, and the
fighting was replaced by negotiations for peace.

The warning also frightened many people by demonstrating
a hard aspect of Dulles's style in dealing with adversaries. He
was not afraid to bring the nation to the brink of war in an effort
to make an opponent "blink" and back off. If the opponent
failed to retreat, Dulles was willing to go to war. This approach
was christened "brinksmanship" and introduced a new word
into the language.

A Partial Success: SEATO

A year after the Korean truce Communism was growing especially strong in Indochina, the Southeast Asian region that embraces today's Vietnam, Laos, and Kampuchea (formerly Cambodia). The United States feared that Communism might reach out from there to the surrounding countries. To forestall this possibility, Dulles set out to unite a collection of nations in a defense pact—a treaty that would create in the Pacific a defense organization like NATO in Europe.

In 1954 he hosted a conference on the proposed pact at Manila, in the Philippines. Attending were delegates from eight nations—Australia, France, Great Britain, New Zealand, Pakistan, the Philippines, Thailand, and the United States. There, agreeing to work together for their mutual security, they signed the agreement that created the South East Asia Treaty Organization (SEATO).

The new body was applauded as a fresh weapon for curbing communist aggression in its region, and Dulles was again admired for his diplomatic skills. Unfortunately, in the long run SEATO turned out to be a disappointment. It never secured long-term military commitments from its members. Nor did they prove willing to help the United States in the Vietnam War. The organization was finally disbanded in 1977.

A Failure: The Suez Crisis

The Dulles venture that failed concerned Egypt. There, President Gamal Abdel Nasser was at war with neighboring Israel, a young nation he hated because he felt it had been founded on lands belonging to the Arabs. When he announced in the mid-1950s that he intended to buy a massive amount of Soviet arms, his words unleashed the widespread fear that he would use them to enlarge the war with Israel.

At the time, Egypt was planning to construct the giant Aswan Dam to control the Nile River's annual flooding and improve the nation's agricultural output. Dulles saw a chance to lure Nasser away from the Soviets. The secretary offered to loan him seventy million dollars for the construction project. But the manuever failed. Nasser continued his plan to buy the Soviets arms. Dulles, tough-minded as ever, angrily withdrew the offer. Angered in his turn, the Egyptian leader retaliated in 1956 by nationalizing the Suez Canal—taking the international waterway for himself.

Ever since the 1880s, the canal had provided the ships of all flags with a time-saving water route between the Mediterranean and the Indian Ocean, and it had been run by an international company. Nasser's takeover caused the worry that his people might not have the technical knowledge to keep it working.

In their anger, Dulles and Nasser plunged the Mideast into what the world press christened "the Suez Crisis." Britain and France were so angered at the possible loss of the canal that they launched a surprise military action with Israel to regain the waterway. The two European powers captured Port Said at its northern terminus, while Israeli troops took a long stretch of land on its eastern bank. But Nasser retaliated by rendering the waterway impassable by blocking it with sunken ships.

The entire Arab world shared Nasser's hatred of Israel, and the Israeli attack on the canal's eastern bank now threatened to plunge the entire Mideast into war. The frightening situation brought about a rare alliance in the United Nations. Both the American and Soviet delegations introduced resolutions calling for a cease-fire and pressed Britain and France to leave the canal area. The two refused to budge. Then Soviet premier Nikita Khrushchev (Stalin had died in 1953) threatened them with a nuclear attack unless they withdrew. His words—along with demonstrations by mobs of angry protesters in London— led to a reluctant departure. The Suez Crisis ended, and the Canal was placed in Egypt's hands.

With his tough-mindeness and "brinksmanship," Dulles was a controversial secretary, praised by many Americans, condemned by many others. But there is no doubt that he was an energetic and dedicated diplomat. During his seven years of service, he traveled nearly a million miles outside the United

··· Dean Rusk ···

States on behalf of the nation's role in the Cold War and other foreign matters.

Dean Rusk and the Cold War

Born February 9, 1909, Dean Rusk was the fourth of five children whose parents trained them always to strive for excellence in whatever they did.[3] It was a training that made a deep impression on Rusk. He achieved mostly As in his early schoolwork and went on to study political science at North Carolina's Davidson College. In the early 1930s he studied political science, economics, and philosophy at Oxford University in England. On returning home, the future secretary began work as an assistant professor of government and international relations at California's Mills College. Four years later, in 1938, he became dean of its faculty.

Rusk embarked on the road that took him to the secretaryship in 1946, when he joined the State Department. In 1950 he was named assistant secretary of state for Far Eastern Affairs and, as such, helped convince the United Nations to intervene in the Korean War. He also worked with future secretary Dulles on the negotiations that brought the formal peace treaty with Japan. He was named secretary of state by President John F. Kennedy in 1961. He found himself serving during one of the hottest years of the Cold War—1962, a year marked by two heated encounters with Cuba.

Two Cuban Problems

The first of the two began in March. That month the United States launched the disastrous Bay of Pigs invasion. The story of the invasion dates back to 1959, when revolutionary leader Fidel Castro, at the end of a long struggle, overthrew the Cuban dictator Batista, a development disliked by the United States because Castro was backed by the Soviet Union. The Central Intelligence Agency (CIA)—which John Foster Dulles's brother, Allan, had helped to found and had headed between 1953 and

1961—trained 1,300 Cuban exiles to invade the country. They were then to incite the island's people to rebel against their new leader. When the invaders were ready to go in 1962, Kennedy opposed the plan, but, since it had been approved by Eisenhower, he reluctantly gave his approval. They landed at Golfo de Cochinos (the Bay of Pigs) and met with disaster. The invaders were repulsed and captured within a few days. The United States later paid Castro fifty-three million dollars in food and medical supplies for their release.

Along with the president, Rusk had opposed the action, certain that it would never work. But, new to his job, he did not oppose it forcefully, and he always felt that by failing to do so, he had served the President poorly. He watched sadly as Kennedy took full responsibility for its failure.

The next problem, the Cuban Missile Crisis, erupted when Kennedy learned that the Soviets were building ballistic missile launching sites in the island country—sites that, located less than 100 miles off Florida, posed an obvious serious danger to the entire United States. The President immediately formed a sixteen-member committee to consider ways of handling the problem. Named to the committee was Rusk.

For a week, the committee considered various possibilities—perhaps to invade Cuba and take the sites, perhaps to bomb them, or perhaps to throw up a naval blockade around the island that would intercept Russian supplies for the sites. It would also cut off all commerical shipping to Cuba and might well starve the island into ordering the Soviets to stop working on the sites.

Of the various possibilities, Rusk favored a naval blockade—or, as it was called, a naval quarantine. When the committee met with the President for a final time, Rusk made his views known. The President nodded and decided on the blockade.

Once the decision was made, the President informed the country of the Cuban situation and, invoking the Monroe Doctrine, said:

It shall be the policy of this nation to regard any nuclear missile launched from Cuba against any nation in the western hemisphere as an attack by the Soviet Union on the United States, requiring full retaliatory reponse upon the Soviet Union.

The announcement brought a hush from one end of the country to the other. The president was ready to go to war with the Soviets over the missile threat. At the same time, he announced that the naval quarantine was in effect. His words came at the very moment when several Russian ships were sailing toward Cuba with supplies for the sites.

The country held its breath. Would the Russian ships press on and meet the American warships in a confrontation that could ignite a Soviet-American nuclear war? Or would they turn back? While waiting for the answer, American troops began preparing to invade Cuba and destroy the sites.

The answer finally came and sent a sigh of relief through the country. At the last moment, the Soviet ships turned around and headed home. The next weeks brought an agreement from Soviet premier Khrushchev to dismantle the sites and remove their missiles from Cuba. The missile crisis had ended in a bloodless victory for the United States.

With that victory, 1962 ended on a high note for the president and his secretary of state. But more successes were soon to come.

The Limited Nuclear Test Ban Treaty

Throughout his time in office, Rusk showed himself to be an opponent of war unless it was unavoidable. He especially feared nuclear warfare, favoring instead the development of conventional arms for the nation's defense. His antinuclear stance led him to what many people remember as his greatest Cold War achievement.

That achievement came in 1963 when he and Kennedy joined Britain's Harold MacMillan in a plea that the prime minister had long made to the world—the plea to end the atmospheric nuclear testing being conducted by the Americans and the Soviets; it threatened havoc by polluting the air and dumping poisonous fallout on countless people. The three men urged a conference with the Soviets to put a stop to the testing. Premier Khrushchev agreed to the meeting.

Beginning in early July, the United States, with Rusk heading its delegation, met in Moscow with British and Soviet representatives. After long talks, they agreed to sign the Limited Nuclear Test Ban Treaty. In the pact, they pledged to do no further testing in the atmospshere, in outer space, and underwater. They were allowed to continue underground testing. The treaty was signed by the three nations on August 5, 1963, with Secretary Rusk signing for the United States.

Eventually, 100 other countries added their signatures to the treaty. The pact did much to ease the tensions of the Cold War. In the next years, other treaties followed it—among them the pacts that came out of the Strategic Arms Limitation Talks in the 1970s and the Intermediate-Range Nuclear Forces Treaty in the 1980s—and helped to lessen those tensions even more.

President Kennedy said that the treaty marked a great "victory for mankind" and might be the crowning achievement of his administration—and of his secretary of state. It was signed just three months before his ill-fated visit to Dallas. Following the assassination, Rusk stayed on under Lyndon B. Johnson and supported the new president in the nation's growing involvement in the Vietnam conflict.

Henry Kissinger and the Cold War

In 1938, when he was in his teens, Henry Kissinger came with his parents to the United States from Furth, Germany, where he had been born on May 27, 1923.[4] The family moved to America to escape Adolf Hitler's brutal treatment of Germany's Jewish population.

In his new country, Kissinger studied political science at Harvard University, became an American citizen in 1943, and interrupted his college work to serve in the army during World War Two. He returned to Harvard at war's end, graduated in

··· Henry Kissinger ···

1950, and earned a doctorate degree in 1954. He then joined
the Harvard faculty as a professor and was soon recognized as
a leading expert on foreign relations and national defense.

In 1969 President Richard M. Nixon appointed Kissinger
as his assistant for national security affairs. As an assistant, he

became Nixon's personal adviser on foreign relations and military policy. And here we come to an odd fact about Kissinger. His most important work was done while he was the president's assistant—years before he was appointed secretary of state.

One of his tasks began to take shape in 1967. That year, during his campaign for the presidency, Nixon indicated that, if elected, he would take steps to end the highly unpopular Vietnam War. On entering the White House, he had Kissinger join in the negotiations that were then being conducted between the United States and North Vietnam in an effort to bring a cease-fire in the conflict. These negotiations had begun during President Lyndon B. Johnson's term in office.

The negotiations proved to be long and arduous. Marked by suspicion on both sides, they dragged on until October 1972, when Kissinger and North Vietnamese representative Le Duc Tho hammered out a cease-fire agreement, only to have it rejected by the South Vietnamese government because of one of its provisions. That provision allowed the North Vietnamese to keep their troops in the south while a final peace was arranged by the warring parties.

The next month saw Nixon win his second bid for the presidency. Determined to free the United States from its entanglement in Vietnam (win the war), he took the drastic step of ordering the bombing of two North Vietnamese cities— Haiphong and the capital, Hanoi. In twelve December days, 36,000 tons of bombs rained on the targets.

The attacks brought results—six days of intensive talks between Kissinger and Le Duc Tho. The talks ended in the Paris Peace Accords—the agreement that the United States would withdraw from Vietnam and that both North and South Vietnam would work together to settle their political problems. An international commission would supervise the cease-fire.

The accords were signed by Kissinger and Le Duc Tho at Paris on January 17, 1973. Unfortunately, the fighting between the North and South continued until 1975. But, for their efforts to end the conflict, Kissinger and Le Duc Tho were chosen to share the prestigious Nobel Peace Prize later in 1973.

Kissinger was appointed secretary of state in September 1973, just eleven months before Nixon's resignation from office in August of the next year. Kissinger went on to serve under President Gerald R. Ford.

The End of the Cold War

When Mikhail Gorbachev assumed the Soviet presidency in 1985, the Cold War began to come to an end.[5] He undertook a sweeping program of political and economic reforms inside the Soviet Union and sought improved relations with the United States and other western nations. His policies led to self-determination for the satellite countries that had stood like fortresses guarding Russia since Stalin's day. By 1990 the Cold War became a thing of the past.

. . .

With the passing of the Cold War, a problem that had dominated the secretary's life for forty years disappeared. But other foreign relations matters quickly came to the forefront and demanded diplomatic attention and participation, among them the Gulf War with Iraq in 1990–1991, the 1991 agreement calling for further reductions in arms by America and the Soviet Union, and the negotiations leading to the 1993 adoption of the North American Free Trade Agreement by the United States, Canada, and Mexico. The secretary, as the nation's ranking diplomat, has always been an important figure on the American scene. With nations everywhere in closer contact today than ever before because of the world's modern communications systems, the secretary of state is destined to become an even more significant figure in the coming years.

SECRETARIES OF STATE
AND THEIR PRESIDENTS
—ROLL CALL—
• • •

George Washington

Thomas Jefferson (1790–1793) organized the State Department and put it on sound footing with an annual budget of less than $10,000. He became the third president of the United States. (See Chapter One.)

Edmund Jennings Randolph (1794–1795), an ardent supporter of the American cause in the Revolutionary War, served as a delegate to the Continental Congress. In 1786 he won election as governor of Virginia and was then assigned to the post of U.S. Attorney General when Washington assumed the presidency in 1789. After Jefferson resigned as secretary of state, Randolph took the office. He was responsible for the eventual signing of the Treaty of San Lorenzo with Spain—a treaty that provided the United States with free navigation of the Spanish-held Mississippi River.

Timothy Pickering (1795–1804) served as colonel of militia and adjutant general to George Washington during the Revolutionary War. Although he opposed Great Britain during the revolution, he supported the maintenance of strong ties with England when the fighting ended. He also urged a strong U.S. army and navy.

John Adams

Timothy Pickering continued as secretary of state in the Adams administration. But because Pickering's foreign policy view favored a close relationship with England, Adams dismissed him from office. Pickering was the only secretary to be discharged for his opposition to his president's policies.

John Marshall (1800–1801) was the oldest of fifteen children. He received no more than a year of formal classroom learning, but was well educated at home by his parents. He fought alongside his father in the Revolutionary War. As secretary of state, he voiced the American position that the neutrality rights of all nations must be strictly observed on the sea. Adams appointed Marshall as chief justice to the Supreme Court in 1801, where he served admirably for thirty-four years.

Thomas Jefferson

James Madison (1801–1809) earned the name "Father of the U.S. Constitution." He arranged the Louisiana Purchase and advanced to the White House, becoming the nation's fourth president. (See Chapter Two.)

James Madison

Robert Smith (1809–1811) was reluctantly appointed by Madison to appease the president's opponents in the

Senate. His overall performance was so inferior that he was dismissed.

James Monroe (1811–1817) served during the War of 1812 between Britain and the United States. He became the nation's fifth president and established the Monroe Doctrine. (See Chapter Three.)

James Monroe

John Quincy Adams (1817–1825) defined the nation's domestic and foreign relations policies in his work on the Monroe Doctrine. He was elected the nation's sixth president. (See Chapter Three.)

John Quincy Adams

Henry Clay (1825–1829) possessed great personal magnetism. He was a major force on the national political scene for over forty years. As secretary, he favored internal improvements, such as linking the east and west by federally financed roads. He oversaw commercial treaties with the Scandinavian countries and advanced good relations with Latin America. Although Clay himself owned slaves, he favored the gradual liberation of the slaves and their eventual resettlement as a free people in Africa.

Andrew Jackson

Martin Van Buren (1829–1831) was known as the "little magician" because of his skill as a politician. He negotiated the treaty with Turkey that gave America commercial access to the Black Sea. He encouraged President Jackson to utilize the "spoils system"—a plan for rewarding supporters with political offices. He became the eighth president of the United States.

Edward Livingston (1831–1833) served as the mayor of New York City in the early 1800s. Because of the dishonesty of a confidential clerk, Livingston found himself indebted to the city government for public funds. He surrendered all his property and resigned his office. By 1826, however, he had repaid the debt plus interest to the New York City government. As secretary of state, he drafted President Jackson's nullification proclamation—the declaration that federal laws supersede state rights.

Louis McLane (1833–1834) joined the U.S. Navy at the age of twelve. He later studied law and began a political career that eventually took him to the U.S. Senate. He also served for a time as U.S. minister to England. President Jackson appointed him secretary of the treasury and then named him secretary of state in 1833. McLane's chief work was the reorganization of the State Department.

John Forsyth (1834–1841) filled several important positions before becoming secretary of state. He was a Georgia senator, a member of the U.S. Congress, and ambassador to Spain. As secretary of state, he helped to obtain reparations from France for American commercial losses during the Napoleonic Wars.

Martin Van Buren

John Forsyth continued as secretary in the Van Buren administration.

William Henry Harrison

Daniel Webster (1841–1843) was reared on a New Hampshire farm. He attended Dartmouth College and became the most highly paid attorney of his time.

Webster was a gifted orator and, as such, had no equal among his contemporaries. He served as Harrison's secretary for just thirty-one days before the president died.

John Tyler

Daniel Webster continued as secretary after Harrison's death. He negotiated the Webster-Ashburton Treaty, which established the border between Maine and Canada's New Brunswick. The treaty also established extradition procedures between England and the United States. He also urged British/American cooperation in an effort to end the international slave trade.

Abel P. Upshur (1843–1844) conducted the first of the negotiations that brought Texas into the Union. While inspecting the warship the USS *Princeton*, along with President Tyler and other dignitaries, Upshur was killed by a cannon, named the "Peacemaker," which exploded during a demonstration firing. Killed along with Secretary Upshur were Secretary of the Navy Thomas W. Gilmer and several others.

John C. Calhoun (1844–1845), the son of a slaveholding farmer, served as a U.S. congressman, secretary of war, senator, vice president, and secretary of state. Calhoun belonged to a group of nationalists, known as the War Hawks, who pressed for war with England to insure America's neutrality at sea. He was also an ardent spokesman for slavery and southern rights. As secretary, he concluded the treaty work begun by Upshur to annex Texas.

James C. Polk

James Buchanan (1845–1849) negotiated the Oregon Treaty. He became the nation's fifteenth president. (See Chapter Four.)

Zachary Taylor

John M. Clayton (1849–1850) opposed the annexation of Texas and the ensuing war with Mexico. As secretary, he negotiated the Clayton-Bulwer Treaty with Great Britain, which stipulated that any Atlantic-Pacific canal built across Central America would be neutral, with neither government exerting complete control over it. The treaty further barred any fortifications along the canal and prohibited colonization of any part of Central America.

Millard Fillmore

Daniel Webster (1850–1852) was the first man to be appointed secretary of state twice. He opposed the annexation of Texas and the war with Mexico, arguing that both opened the way to the expansion of slavery into the far West. He supported the Fugitive Slave Act, which empowered federal commissioners to force citizens to help capture runaway slaves. Although his support of this act angered antislavery forces, it helped to preserve the Union.

Edward Everett (1852–1853) served only four months as secretary. He opposed the British and French idea of having the United States sign a pact renouncing forever the acquisition of Cuba. He asked if Britain or France would promote such a pact if Cuba were located at the entrance of the Thames or the Seine.

Franklin Pierce

William L. Marcy (1853–1857) helped negotiate the Gadsden Purchase from Mexico. The purchase, needed as a route for a proposed southern transcontinental railroad, covered a 29,000-square-mile strip of land located in the present-day states of New Mexico and

Arizona. Marcy was an ardent expansionist and favored the annexation of Cuba.

James Buchanan

Lewis Cass (1857–1860) was popularly known as a "doughface," a name associated with northerners who supported southern measures in order to keep peace. He resigned in protest over Buchanan's refusal to reinforce Fort Moultrie, S.C., even though secessionists threatened to take over the federal fort.

Jeremiah S. Black (1860–1861) ordered diplomats abroad to dissuade foreign governments from recognizing the Confederacy as an independent state if war between the North and South broke out. He also urged President Buchanan to place troops in southern forts to prevent their being taken over by the secessionists.

Abraham Lincoln

William H. Seward (1861–1869) demanded a loyalty oath of all federal employees and dismissed those who were sympathetic to the South. (See Chapter Five.)

Andrew Johnson

William H. Seward continued in the Johnson administration. An ardent expansionist, he negotiated the purchase of Alaska, dubbed "Seward's Ice Box," and annexed Midway Island in the Pacific.

Ulysses S. Grant

Elihu B. Washburne (1869) served from March fifth to the sixteenth. He resigned to become minister to France.

Hamilton Fish (1869–1877) reorganized the State Department. He negotiated the Treaty of Washington, which was a claim against Great Britain for damages inflicted on Union ships during the Civil War by vessels built in Liverpool and sold to the Confederacy.

Rutherford B. Hayes

William M. Evarts (1877–1881) negotiated the Treaty of 1880, which put a halt to Chinese immigration to the United States for a limited time. Although the French were trying to construct a canal across the Isthmus of Panama at this time, Evarts urged the policy that the United States have control over any waterway built in Panama. President Hayes announced this policy to Congress in 1880.

James Garfield

James G. Blaine (1881) resigned after the assassination of President Garfield. He served too brief a time to allow him to establish his views on foreign policy.

Chester A. Arthur

F. T. Frelinghuysen (1881–1885) held several political offices, among them Newark's city attorney, New Jersey's attorney general, and U.S. Senator. As secretary of state, he favored closer commercial relations with Latin America. He negotiated a treaty with Hawaii that gave the United States a naval base at Pearl Harbor.

Grover Cleveland

Thomas F. Bayard (1885–1889) tried to arbitrate a U.S. conflict with Canada and Great Britain over fishing rights in the Atlantic and fur sealing rights in the Pacific. The arbitration ended in a treaty that the Senate refused to ratify.

Benjamin Harrison

James G. Blaine (1889–1892) taught school as an instructor in mathematics and, later, as an instructor at the Pennsylvania Institute for the Blind. His political career covered terms in the U.S. House of Representatives and Senate. As secretary of state, he attempted to foster goodwill and cooperation between North and South America. He served as chairman of the first Pan-American conference, where he hoped to encourage among the nations a system of arbitration for preventing future wars in the Western Hemisphere.

James G. Blaine remained as secretary of state in President Harrison's cabinet. He continued to seek better relations with Latin America.

John W. Foster (1892–1893), a lawyer, concentrated on international cases in Washington, representing foreign legations before commissions and arbitration boards. As secretary, he was eager to annex Hawaii and quietly encouraged the uprising that saw American sugar and pineapple growers on the island overthrow the government of Queen Liliuokalani. He then had President Harrison present to Congress a treaty for annexation of Hawaii.

Grover Cleveland

William Q. Gresham (1893–1895), a modest man of deep integrity, was respected and liked by both his friends and political enemies. His integrity showed itself when he strongly opposed the takeover of the

Hawaiian Islands by the group of American sugar and pineapple growers. He condemned the Americans for their action and successfully urged President Cleveland to withdraw the treaty that had been presented to Congress on their behalf for the annexation of Hawaii. The treaty, which had been presented to Congress by President Harrison, was still under consideration when Cleveland entered the White House. Hawaii was later made a U.S. territory during the Spanish-American War.

Richard Olney (1895–1897) proved to be an aggressive and opinionated secretary of state. He defended the Monroe Doctrine in a long-running boundary dispute between Venezuela and Great Britain's colony of Guiana. He stated that intervention by the United States was permissible under the Monroe Doctrine and declared that the "United States was practically sovereign on this continent." An arbitration commission later settled the dispute.

William McKinley

John Sherman (1897–1898) was best known for his financial expertise. He served in the political arena as a U.S. representative, senator, and secretary of treasury. When named secretary of state, he opposed the United States going to war with Spain over its inhumane treatment of the Cuban people.

William R. Day (1898) held the office of secretary of state for only six months before resigning. He then became chairman of the United States peace commissioners who met in Paris to negotiate the treaty with Spain at the end of the Spanish-American War.

John M. Hay (1898–1905) favored annexation of the Philippines. He championed the "Open Door policy" for China. He sent American troops to China in the international effort to rescue the foreign legations caught up in the Boxer rebellion.

Theodore Roosevelt

John M. Hay concluded treaties with Great Britain and Panama that made the construction of the Panama Canal possible. (See Chapter Six.)

Elihu Root (1905–1909) undertook a significant tour through Central and South America soon after being named secretary of state. At the time, Theodore Roosevelt was the target of widespread Latin anger because, invoking the Monroe Doctrine, he had ordered the United States to supervise the financial affairs of several Caribbean countries that were deeply in debt to a number of foreign nations. Though he said he had done this to keep the creditor nations from taking over the Caribbean countries, his actions infuriated much of Central and South America. Root greatly soothed their angers and did much to reduce tensions throughout the hemisphere. For his Central and South American efforts—and for other work that helped promote world harmony—he was awarded the Nobel Peace Prize in 1912.

Robert Bacon (1909) served under Roosevelt from January to March of 1909. Then the newly elected President Taft appointed him Ambassador to France.

William Howard Taft

Philander C. Knox (1909–1913) represented many large organizations such as the Carnegie Company. Knox served as attorney general of the United States and senator from Pennsylvania. As secretary, he reorganized the State Department. In foreign affairs Knox's goal was to protect U.S. financial interests in Latin

America, China, and Japan, often at the expense of friendly cultural relations.

Woodrow Wilson

William Jennings Bryan (1913–1915) was a major force in American politics for three decades, serving in the U.S. House of Representatives and Senate. As secretary, he advocated U.S. neutrality, including restrictions against American travel on belligerent vessels and the prohibition of loans to Britain and France. He resigned in protest over Wilson's strong note to Germany following the sinking of the liner *Lusitania,* by a German U-boat.

Robert Lansing (1915–1920) arranged for the purchase of the U.S. Virgin Islands from Denmark. He advocated U.S. involvement in World War One. At the Paris Peace Conference, Lansing disagreed with Wilson's provision concerning the establishment of the League of Nations. Also, in Lansing's opinion, the Treaty of Versailles was too harsh on Germany. When the president suffered a stroke, Lansing called a cabinet meeting on his own authority. This was the final straw for Wilson, and he asked for Lansing's resignation.

Bainbridge Colby (1920–1921) set forth the policy that refused U.S. recognition of the Soviet Union after the 1917 Russian Revolution.

Warren G. Harding

Charles Evans Hughes (1921–1925) organized and chaired the Washington Conference that called for an international reduction in armaments. He improved relations with Latin America. (See Chapter Seven.)

Calvin Coolidge

Charles Evans Hughes served briefly under Coolidge and then resigned to return to private law practice. He was appointed Chief Justice of the U.S. Supreme Court in 1930. (See Chapter Seven.)

Frank B. Kellogg (1925–1929) negotiated the Kellogg-Briand Pact of 1928, in which fifteen countries— among them Great Britain, France, Germany, Japan, and Australia—agreed to renounce war as a means of settling international disputes. For his efforts on behalf of the treaty, Kellogg was awarded the 1929 Nobel Peace Prize.

Herbert Hoover

Henry L. Stimson (1929–1933) enunciated the Stimson Doctrine, a declaration stating that the United States would not recognize territorial changes brought about by force. This was in response to Japan's occupation of Manchuria in 1931.

Franklin D. Roosevelt

Cordell Hull (1933–1944) was instrumental in the founding of the United Nations. He implemented Roosevelt's Good Neighbor policy toward Latin America. He was awarded the Nobel Peace Prize in 1945.

Edward R. Stettinius, Jr. (1944–1945) hosted the Dumbarton Conference that paved the way for the establishment of the United Nations. He then led the United States delegation to the founding conference of the United Nations in San Francisco. (See Chapter Eight.)

Harry S. Truman

Edward R. Stettinius, Jr. was a holdover from the Roosevelt administration. He resigned to become the U.S. representative to the United Nations.

James F. Byrnes (1945–1947) participated in the decision to use the atomic bomb to end the war with Japan. He was opposed to postwar Soviet expansion.

George C. Marshall (1947–1949) developed the European Recovery Program, or Marshall Plan. He was awarded the Nobel Peace Prize in 1953. (See Chapter Nine.)

Dean G. Acheson (1949–1953) supported the formation of the North Atlantic Treaty Organization, in which twelve countries adopted a pact whereby an aggressive attack on one would be an attack on all. He advocated the Truman Doctrine's "containment policy" to thwart the expansion of communism. (See Chapter Ten.)

Dwight D. Eisenhower

John Foster Dulles (1951–1959) helped Eisenhower end the Korean War and hosted the conference that resulted in the formation of the South East Asia Treaty Organization (SEATO). SEATO was intended as a deterrent to the spread of communism in Southeast Asia. (See Chapter Ten.)

Christian A. Herter (1959–1961) participated in the diplomatic efforts to have pilot Francis Gary Powers returned to the United States after his high-altitude U-2 reconnaissance plane was brought down inside the Soviet Union in 1960. Soviet Premier Nikita Khrushchev accused the United States of using the plane to spy on his country and demanded an apology, which Eisenhower refused to give. In 1962 Powers was returned home in exchange for Soviet spy Colonel Rudolf Abel.

John F. Kennedy

Dean Rusk (1961–1969) urged—and won—approval for blockading the shipment of Soviet missile equipment to Cuba during the Cuban Missile Crisis of 1962. He signed the Nuclear Test Ban Treaty of 1963 with the Soviet Union and Great Britain. (See Chapter Ten.)

Lyndon B. Johnson

Dean Rusk remained as secretary for Johnson and supported U.S. involvement in Vietnam. He favored educational and cultural exchanges with Communist China, but opposed diplomatic relations with Communist China as well as the country's admission to the United Nations.

Richard M. Nixon

William P. Rogers (1969–1973) accompanied President Nixon on his trip to Communist China in 1972. The journey opened the way to improved relations between China and the United States. Rogers recommended international cooperation to combat terrorism.

Henry Kissinger (1973–1977) worked toward easing tensions with the Soviet Union. Before being named secretary, he negotiated the 1973 Paris Peace Treaty that ended the Vietnam War. Along with North Vietnamese representative Le Duc Tho, Kissinger was awarded the Nobel Peace Prize in 1973 for his efforts in ending the conflict. (See Chapter Ten.)

Gerald R. Ford

Henry Kissinger continued as secretary in the Ford administration and obtained a peace agreement between Egypt and Israel.

Jimmy Carter

Cyrus R. Vance (1977–1980) negotiated with the Soviets for the mutual reduction of strategic arms. He favored an easing of tensions between the United States and the Soviet Union.

Edmund S. Muskie (1980–1981) worked to free the foreign nationalists who were taken prisoner by Iran's Ayatollah Khomeini in 1979 and held hostage for 444 days.

Ronald Reagan

Alexander M. Haig, Jr. (1981–1982) tried and failed to find a peaceful solution to the British-Argentine dispute over the ownership of the Falkland Islands, a dispute that ended in a brief war.

George F. Shultz (1982–1989) denied an entry visa to Palestine Liberation Organization chairman Yasser Arafat to speak to the United Nations because Arafat condoned terrorism. After the Palestine leader recanted terrorism and conceded Israel's right to exist, the administration allowed him to enter the country and speak before the United Nations.

George Bush

James A. Baker (1989–1992) urged the reunification of East and West Germany into one nation after the collapse of the Soviet Union. He advanced the possibility of a settlement of the Arab-Israeli conflict. He resigned to manage President Bush's reelection campaign.

Lawrence S. Eagleburger (1992–1993) a career diplomat, served for only three months after replacing Baker. He had been Baker's chief deputy.

Bill Clinton

Warren Christopher (1993–) pressed the Mexican government to take steps to assure a fair national election in August 1994. He assisted in arranging peace between warring Israel and Jordan and worked with Clinton for the adoption of the North American Free Trade Agreement with Canada and Mexico.

SOURCE NOTES
● ● ●

Chapter One Meet the Secretary of State

1. The United States Department of State, *A Short History of the Department of State*, 1781–1981 (Washington, D.C.: 1981), 3, 4.

2. D. S. Muzzey, *History of Our Country* (Boston: Ginn, 1941), 188.

3. *History of Our Country*, 189.

4. W. A. Degregorio, *The Complete Book of U. S. Presidents* (New York: Barricade Books, 1993), 9.

5. The material in the section "The Secretary of State" is developed from: R. Famighetti, ed., *The World Almanac and Book of Facts 1994* (New York: Funk & Wagnalls, 1993), 837–839; A. Nevins and H. S. Commager, *A Short History of the United States* (New York: The Modern Library, 1969), 554–555; W. Ruoff, ed., *The Standard Dictionary of Facts* (Buffalo: Frontier Press, 1916), 636; *A Short History of the U.S. Department of State*, 10.

6. The material in the section "The Secretaries of State: A Varied History" is developed from: *The Complete Book of U.S. Presidents*, 252, 383, 519.

Chapter Two James Madison and Napoleon's Bargain

1. J. A. Garraty, *The American Nation: A History of the United States* (New York: Harper & Row, 1966), 176.
2. The biographical material on Secretary Madison is developed from: W. A. Degregorio, *The Complete Book of U.S. Presidents* (New York: Barricade Books, 1993), 55, 56, 57, 58; J. D. Hicks, *The Federal Union: A History of the United States to 1865*, 2d ed. (Boston: Houghton Mifflin, 1952), 185, 195.
3. The material in the section "Madison and the Louisiana Purchase" is developed from: T. A. Bailey, *The American Pageant: A History of the Republic* (Boston: D. C. Heath, 1956), 189, 190; J. D. Hicks, *A Short History of American Democracy* (Boston: Houghton Mifflin, 1949), 159; Hicks, *The Federal Union: A History of the United States to 1865* (Boston: Houghton Mifflin, 1952), 262–263; H. Thomas, *A History of the World* (New York: Harper & Row, 1979), 513–514.

Chapter Three John Quincy Adams and the Monroe Doctrine

1. The material in the section "John Quincy Adams," including the subsection "Florida Joins the United States," is developed from: R. N. Current, H. T. Williams, and F. Freidel, *American History: A Survey* (New York: Knopf, 1963), 215; W. A. Degregorio, *The Complete Book of U.S. Presidents* (New York: Barricade Books, 1993), 48–51, 89–90; J. C. Estrin, *American History Made Simple* (Garden City: Doubleday, 1968), 62–63; J. D. Hicks, *A Short History of American Democracy* (Boston: Houghton Mifflin, 1849), 206.

2. The material in the section "Adams and the Monroe Doctrine" is developed from: S. F. Bemis, *John Quincy Adams and the Union* (New York: Knopf, 1956), 545; K. C. Davis, *Don't Know Much About History* (New York: Avon, 1990), 113; F. Escher, Jr., *A Brief History of the United States* (London: English Universities Press, 1956), 76–77; J. A. Garraty, *The American Nation: A History of the United States* (New York: Harper & Row, 1966), 207; J. A. Garraty and P. Gay, eds., *The Columbia History of the World* (New York: Harper & Row, 1972), 797–798; *A Short History of American Democracy*, 209; *American History: A Survey*, 229; *The Complete Book of U.S. Presidents*, 101; *American History Made Simple*, 62.

Chapter Four James Buchanan, Oregon Country, and a War with Mexico

1. The material in the section "James Buchanan" is developed from: W. A. Degregorio, *The Complete Book of U.S. Presidents* (New York: Barricade Books, 1993) 211–213; J. D. Hicks, *A Short History of American Democracy* (Boston: Houghton Mifflin, 1949) 349.

2. The material in the section "Buchanan and Oregon County" is developed from: B. DeVoto, *The Year of Decision, 1846* (Boston: Little Brown, 1943), 104; J. A. Garraty, *The American Nation: A History of the United States* (New York: Harper & Row, 1966), 317–318; J. D. Hicks, *The Federal Union: A History of the United States to 1865* (Boston: Houghton Mifflin, 1952), 476.

3. The material in the section "Buchanan, Texas, and New Mexico" is developed from: M. Burke, *United States History: The Growth of Our Land,* (Chicago: American Technical Society, 1957) 98–101; K. C. Davis, *Don't Know Much About History* (New York: Avon, 1990), 139–140; W. J. Jacobs, *War With Mexico* (Brookfield, Connecticut: Millbrook Press, 1993), 37, 39; R. Leckie, *The Wars of America*, Vol. 1 (New York: HarperCollins, 1992), 340; J. Morgan, *Our Presidents* (New York: Macmillan, 1958), 101; A. Nevins and H. S. Commager, *A Short*

History of the United States, (New York: The Modern Library, 1969), 220; *The Year of Decision,* 139–140.

4. *A Short History of American Democracy,* 340.

Chapter Five William Henry Seward and His "Ice Box"

1. The biographical material in the section "William Henry Seward," including his use of the Monroe Doctrine during the Civil War, is developed from: T. A. Bailey, *The American Pageant: A History of the Republic* (Boston: D. C. Heath, 1956), 408, 417, 440; M. Cunliffe, *American Presidents and the Presidency* (New York: American Heritage Press, 1972), 284; T. K. Lothrop, *William Henry Seward* (Boston: Houghton Mifflin, 1899), 193, 289, 411–412; S. E. Morison and H. S. Commager, *The Growth of the American Republic,* Vol. 2 (New York: Oxford University Press, 1950), 60.

2. The material in the section "Seward and His Alaska 'Ice Box'" is developed from: J. A. Garraty, *The American Nation: A History of the United States* (New York: Harper & Row, 1966), 622; J. D. Hicks, *A Short History of American Democracy* (Boston: Houghton Mifflin, 1949), 404, 612; *The Growth of the American Republic,* 60–61; *William Henry Seward,* 393, 526–534, 541, 543, 544, 549; *The American Pageant,* 480–481.

Chapter Six John M. Hay, China, and the Panama Canal

1. The material in the section "John M. Hay" is developed from: W. A. Degregorio, *The Complete Book of U.S. Presidents* (New York: Barricade Books, 1993), 365; J. A. Krout, *The United States Since 1865* (New York: Barnes & Noble, 1962), 96.

2. The material in the section "The Spanish-American War" is developed from: T. A. Bailey, *The American Pageant:*

A History of the Republic (Boston: D. C. Heath, 1956), 621–622; E. F. Dolan and M. M. Scariano, *Cuba and the United States: Troubled Neighbors* (New York: Franklin Watts, 1987), 38–41; J. C. Estrin, *American History Made Simple* (Garden City: Doubleday, 1968) 131; J. A. Garraty and P. Gay, eds., *The Columbia History of the World* (New York: Harper & Row, 1972), 936; S. E. Morison and H. S. Commager, *The Growth of the American Republic* (New York: Oxford University Press, 1950), 329, 331–335.

3. The material in the section "Hay and the 'Open Door' for China" is developed from: M. Burke, *United States History: The Growth of Our Land* (Chicago: American Technical Society, 1957), 144–145; R. N. Current, H. T. Williams and F. Freidel, *American History: A Survey* (New York: Knopf, 1963), 538, 558; N. A. Graebner, ed., *An Uncertain Tradition: American Secretaries of State in the Twentieth Century* (New York: McGraw-Hill, 1961), 49; J. D. Hicks, *A Short History of American Democracy* (Boston: Houghton Mifflin, 1949), 621–623; *The American Pageant*, 631–633, 645–647.

4. The material in the section "Hay and the Panama Canal" is developed from: R. N. Current, H. T. Williams, and F. Freidel, *American History: A Survey* (New York: Knopf, 1963), 318; E. F. Dolan, *Panama and the United States: Their Canal, Their Stormy Years* (New York: Franklin Watts, 1990), 63–65; The United States Since 1865, 96–97, 119–120.

Chapter Seven Charles Evans Hughes and the Quest for World Peace

1. The material on President Wilson's fourteen points for world peace and U.S. objections to the League of Nations provision in the fourteenth point is developed from: E. Foner and J. A. Garraty, eds., *The Reader's Companion to American History* (Boston: Houghton Mifflin, 1991), 526; N. A. Graebner, ed., *An Uncertain Tradition: American Secretaries of State in the Twentieth Century* (New York: McGraw-Hill, 1961), 146–147; J. A. S. Grenville, *A History of the World in the Twentieth*

Century (Cambridge, Massachusetts: Harvard University Press, 1994), 131–132; S. E. Morison and H. S. Commager, *The Growth of the American Republic,* Vol. 2 (New York: Oxford University Press, 1950), 494.

2. The material in the section "Charles Evans Hughes" is developed from: W. A. Degregorio, *The Complete Book of U.S. Presidents* (New York: Barricade Books, 1993), 417–418; *The Reader's Companion to American History,* 525–526.

3. The material in the section "Hughes and the Quest for World Peace" is developed from: M. Burke, *United States History: The Growth of Our Land* (Chicago: American Technical Society, 1957), 169–170; J. D. Hicks, *A Short History of American Democracy* (Boston: Houghton Mifflin, 1949), 714–718; United States Department of State, *A Short History of the U.S. Department of State, 1781–1981* (Washington, D.C.: The United States Department of State, 1981), 27; *An Uncertain Tradition,* 139–140, 141.

Chapter Eight Edward R. Stettinius and the United Nations

1. The material on the early plans for the United Nations is developed from: M. Burke, United States History: The Growth of Our Land (Chicago: American Technical Society, 1957), 195–197; J. A. Garraty and P. Gay, eds., *The Columbia History of the World* (New York: Harper & Row, 1981), 1071; S. E. Morison and H. S. Commager, *The Growth of the American Republic,* Vol. 2 (New York: Oxford University Press, 1950), 810, 814–815.

2. The material in the section "Edward R. Stettinius" is developed from: N. A. Graebner, ed., *An Uncertain Tradition: American Secretaries of State in the Twentieth Century* (New York: McGraw-Hill, 1961), 210–211, 213–215.

3. The material on the section "Stettinius and the United Nations," including the subsections "The Dumbarton Oaks Proposals" and "The San Francisco Conference," is developed

from: J. A. Krout, *The United States Since 1865* (New York: Barnes and Noble, 1962), 219; A. Nevins and H. S. Commager, *A Short History of the United States* (New York: The Modern Library, 1969), 534–535; *The Columbia History of the World,* 1071; *United States History,* 197–203; *An Uncertain Tradition,* 215–218, 220, 22.

Chapter Nine George C. Marshall and a Torn Europe

1. The material in the section "George C. Marshall" is developed from E. Cray, ed., *General of the Army, Soldier and Statesman* (New York: W. W. Norton, 1990), 110, 111, 450, 555; N. A. Graebner, ed., *An Uncertain Tradition: Secretaries of State in the Twentieth Century* (New York: McGraw-Hill, 1961), 245–246; J. A. Grenville, *A History of the World in the Twentieth Century* (Cambridge, Massachusetts: Harvard University Press, 1994), 347; A Rothe, ed., *Current Biography 1947* (New York: H. W. Wilson, 1848), 424, 425, 426, 427.

2. The material in the section "Marshall and the Truman Doctrine" is developed from: D. McCullough, Truman (New York: Simon & Schuster, 1992), 546, 547–548; J. D. Hicks, *A Short History of American Democracy* (Boston: Houghton Mifflin, 1949), 890–891; A. Nevins and H. S. Commager, *A Short History of the United States* (New York: The Modern Library, 1969), 546; *An Uncertain Tradition,* 252.

3. The material in the section "Marshall and a Torn Europe" is developed from: K. Davis, *Don't Know Much About History* (New York: Avon, 1990), 322; E. Foner and J. A. Garraty, eds., *The Reader's Companion to American History* (Boston: Houghton Mifflin, 1991), 703; J. A. Garraty and P. Gay, eds., *The Columbia History of the World* (New York: Harper & Row, 1972), 1076; *A Short History of the United States,* 547–548; Truman, 562–563; *A History of the World in the Twentieth Century,* 382–383; *A Short History of American Democracy,* 891–893; *An Uncertain Tradition,* 245, 255.

Chapter Ten Four Secretaries and the Cold War

1. The material in the section "Dean Acheson and the Cold War" is developed from E. Foner and J. A. Garraty, eds., *The Reader's Companion to American History* (Boston: Houghton Mifflin, 1991), 6–7; J. A. Garraty and P. Gay, *The Columbia History of the World* (New York: Harper & Row, 1972, 1090; J. A. S. Grenville, *A History of the World in the Twentieth Century* (Cambridge, Massachusetts: Harvard University Press, 1994), 381, 382, 391; F. N. Magill, ed., *Great Lives from History*, American Series, Vol. 1 (Englewood Cliffs, New Jersey: Salem Press, 1987), 1, 2, 3, 4; A. Rothe, ed., *Current Biography 1949* (New York: H. W. Wilson, 1950), 2–5; M. Block, Ed., *Current Biography 1941* (New York: H. W. Wilson, 1941), 6–7.

2. The material in the section "John Foster Dulles and the Cold War," including the subsections "A Success: Halting the Korean War," "A Partial Success: SEATO," and "A Failure: The Suez Crisis," is developed from: M. Burke, *United States History, the Growth of Our Land* (Chicago: American Technical Society, 1957), 432, 440–441; D. Halberstam, *The Fifties* (New York: Villard, 1993), 394–395, 396–397; L. Mosley, *Dulles: A Biography of Eleanor, Allen, and John Foster Dulles and Their Family Network* (New York: Dial Press/James Wade, 1978), 255–256, 259–261, 395; A Nevins and H. S. Commager, *A Short History of the United States* (New York: The Modern Library, 1966), 598–599, 605–606, 607; S. E. Morison, *The Oxford History of the American People*, Vol. 3 (New York: New American Library, 1972), 465–467; *The Columbia History of the World*, 1080, 1102.

3. The material in the section "Dean Rusk and the Cold War," including the subsections "Two Cuban Problems" and "The Limited Nuclear Test Ban Treaty," is developed from: W. A. Degregorio, *The Complete Book of U.S. Presidents* (New York: Barricade Books, 1993), 557–558, 572; C. Moritz, ed., *Current Biography 1961* (New York: H. W. Wilson, 1962), 402, 403; D. Rusk, *As I Saw It* (New York: W. W. Norton, 1990), 230–242;

The Oxford History of the American People, 496; *A Short History of the United States,* 638–640.

4. The material in the section "Henry Kissinger and the Cold War" is developed from: E. F. Dolan, MIA: Missing in Action (New York: Franklin Watts, 1989), 27–28; W. Isaacson, *Kissinger* (New York: Simon & Schuster, 1992), 36, 68, 102, 588, 590; R. Leckie, *The Wars of America,* Vol. 2 (New York: HarperCollins, 1992), 1037–1038; *The Complete Book of American Presidents,* 593; *The Reader's Companion to American History,* 1036.

5. The material in the section "The End of the Cold War" is developed from: J. A. Garraty, *1001 Things Everyone Should Know About American History* (New York: Doubleday, 1989), 38; R. Famighetti, ed., *The World Almanac and Book of Facts 1994* (New York: Funk & Wagnalls, 1993), 707; O. Johnson, exec. ed., *The 1993 Information Please Almanac* (New York: Houghton Mifflin, 1992), 121, 253; *The Complete Book of U.S. Presidents,* 596, 628, 657–58, 693.

BIBLIOGRAPHY

•••

Bailey, Thomas A. *The American Pageant: A History of the Republic.* Boston: D.C. Heath, 1956.

Banfield, Susan. *James Madison.* New York: Franklin Watts, 1986.

Bemis, Samuel Flagg. *John Quincy Adams and the Union.* NewYork: Knopf, 1956.

Block, Maxine, ed. *Current Biography 1940.* New York: H. W. Wilson, 1940.

Current Biography 1941. New York: H. W. Wilson, 1941.

Burke, Merle. *United States History: The Growth of Our Land.* Chicago: American Technical Society, 1957.

Candee, Marjorie Dent, ed. *Current Biography 1953.* New York: The H. W. Wilson Company, 1954.

Carruth, Gorton. *The Encyclopedia of American Facts & Dates,* 9th ed. New York: Harper & Row, 1987.

Cunliffe, Marcus. *American Presidents and the Presidency.* New York: American Heritage Press, 1972.

Cray, Ed. *General of the Army: Soldier and Statesman.* New York: W. W. Norton, 1990.

Current, Richard N., Harry T. Williams and Frank Freidel. *American History: A Survey.* New York: Knopf, 1963.

Davis, Kenneth C. *Don't Know Much About History.* New York: Avon, 1990.

Degregorio, William A. *The Complete Book of U.S. Presidents.* New York: Barricade Books, 1993.

DeVoto, Bernard. *The Year of Decision: 1846.* Boston: Little, Brown, 1943.

Dolan, Edward F. *Panama and the United States: Their Canal, Their Stormy Years.* New York: Franklin Watts, 1990.
America After Vietnam. New York: Franklin Watts, 1989.

Dolan, Edward F. and Margaret M. Scariano. *Cuba and the United States: Troubled Neighbors.* New York: Franklin Watts, 1987.

Escher, Franklin, Jr. *A Brief History of the United States.* London: English Universities Press, 1956.

Estrin, Jack C. *American History Made Simple.* Garden City, New York: Doubleday, 1968.

Famaghetti, Robert, ed. *The World Almanac and Book of Facts, 1994.* New York: Funk & Wagnalls, 1993.

Foner, Eric and John A. Garraty, eds. *The Reader's Companion to American History.* Boston: Houghton Mifflin, 1991.

Garraty, John A. *The American Nation: A History of the United States.* New York: Harper & Row, 1966.
1001 Things Everyone Should Know About American History. New York: Doubleday, 1989.
Woodrow Wilson: A Great Life in Brief. New York: Knopf, 1956.

Garraty, John A. and Peter Gay, eds. *The Columbia History of the World.* New York: Harper & Row, 1972.

Graebner, Norman A., ed. *An Uncertain Tradition: American Secretaries of State in the Twentieth Century.* New York: McGraw-Hill, 1961.

Halberstam, David. *The Fifties.* New York: Villard, 1993.

Hicks, John D. *The Federal Union: A History of the United States to 1865.* Boston: Houghton Mifflin, 1952.

A Short History of American Democracy. Boston: Houghton Mifflin, 1949.

Hunt, Michael H. *Ideology and U.S. Foreign Policy.* New Haven and London: Yale University Press, 1987.

Isaacson, Walter. *Kissinger.* New York: Simon & Schuster, 1992.

Jacobs, W. J. *War with Mexico.* Brookfield, Connecticut: Millbrook Press, 1993.

Johnson, Otto, exec. ed. *The 1993 Information Please Almanac.* Boston: Houghton Mifflin, 1992.

Krout, John A. *United States to 1865.* New York: Barnes & Noble, 1962.

Leckie, Robert. *The Wars of America.* New York: Harper & Row, 1981.

The Wars of America, Vol. 1. New York: HarperCollins, 1992.

Lothrop, Thornton Kirkland. *William Henry Seward.* Boston and New York: Houghton Mifflin, 1899.

Magill, Frank N., ed. *Great Lives from History,* American Series, Vol. 1. Englewood Cliffs, New Jersey: Salem Press, 1987.

McCullough, David. *Truman.* New York: Simon & Schuster, 1992.

Morgan, James. *Our Presidents.* New York: Macmillan, 1958.

Morison, Samuel Eliot. *The Oxford History of the American People,* Vol. 3. New York: New American Library, 1972.

Morison, Samuel Eliot and Henry Steele Commager. *The Growth of the American Republic,* Vol. 2. New York: Oxford University Press, 1950.

Moritz, Charles, ed. *Current Biography 1961.* New York: H. W. Wilson, 1962.

Current Biography 1972. New York: H. W. Wilson, 1973.

Mosley, Leonard. *Dulles: A Biography of Eleanor, Allen, and John Foster Dulles and Their Family Network.* New York: The Dial Press/James Wade, 1978.

Muzzey, David Saville. *A History of Our Country.* Boston: Ginn, 1941.

Nevins, Allan and Henry Steele Commager. *A Short History of the United States.* New York: Knopf, Inc. and Washington Square Press, 1966.

The Oxford Dictionary of Quotations, 3rd ed. New York: Oxford University Press, 1980.

Roberts, J. M. *History of the World.* New York: Oxford University Press, 1993.

Rothe, Anna, ed. *Current Biography 1947.* New York: H. W. Wilson, 1948.

Current Biography 1949. New York: H. W. Wilson, 1950.

Ruoff, Henry W., ed. *The Standard Dictionary of Facts.* Buffalo: Frontier Press, 1916.

Rusk, Dean (as told to Richard Rusk). *As I Saw It.* New York: W. W. Norton, 1990.

Thomas, Hugh. *A History of the World.* New York: Harper & Row, 1979.

United States Department of State. *A Short History of the U.S. Department of State, 1781–1981.* Washington, D.C.: U. S. Government Printing Office, 1981.

Van Deusen, Glyndon G. *William Henry Seward.* New York: Oxford University Press, 1967.

INDEX

• • •

Kellogg-Briand Pact, 105–106

Kennedy, John F., 10, 79, 85, 86, 88, 107

Kissinger, Henry, 75, 77, 88–91, 89, 108, 109

Knox, Philander C., 104

Korean War, 11, 75, 78–79, 80–81, 82, 85, 107

Lansing, Robert, 40, 79, 105

League of Nations, 54, 56, 59, 61, 63, 105

Lincoln, Abraham, 38, 39, 40, 45, 100

Livingston, Edward, 96

Livingston, Robert, 18

Louisiana Purchase, 13–19, 21, 24, 34, 94

McKinley, William, 45, 50, 103

McLane, Louis, 96

Madison, James, 8, 11, 14–19, 15, 21, 25, 27, 36, 94–95

Marcy, William L., 99

Marshall, George C., 11, 68–75, 69, 78, 107

Marshall, John, 94

Marshall Plan, 11, 73–75, 78, 107

Mexican War, 27, 32–34

Mexico, 27, 31–35, 38–39, 91, 110

Monroe, James, 18, 23, 25, 27, 53, 95

Monroe Doctrine, 20, 24–26, 30, 39, 73, 86, 95, 102, 103, 104

Muskie, Edmund S., 109

New Mexico territory, 27, 32–34

Nixon, Richard M., 89, 90, 91, 108

Nobel Peace Prize, 75, 90, 104, 106, 107, 108

North American Free Trade Agreement, 91, 110

North Atlantic Treaty Organizations (NATO), 10, 78–79, 107

Nuclear test ban treaties, 87–88, 108

Olney, Richard, 102

Oregon Country, the, 27, 30–31, 34, 98

Oregon Treaty, 98

Panama Canal, 11, 41, 44, 50, 100, 103

Paris Peace Conference, 105

Paris Peace Treaty, 1973, 90, 108

Philippines, the, 46–48, 80, 82, 103

Pickering, Timothy, 94

Pierce, Franklin, 99

Polk, James C., 27, 29, 30, 32, 34, 98

Randolph, Edmund Jennings, 93

Reagan, Ronald, 109